PINE FURNITURE PROJECTS

FOR THE HOME

DAVE MACKENZIE

Guild of Master Craftsman Publications Ltd

First published 1997 by
Guild of Master Craftsman Publications Ltd,
166 High Street, Lewes, East Sussex BN7 1XU

Reprinted 1997, 1998

ISBN 1 86108 035 2

Photography © Dave Mackenzie,
except photographs on pages 28, 29, 30, 37, 50, 57,
66, 72, 81, 90, 95, 102, 107, and 114, by Ray Highnam
Illustrations © Dave Mackenzie

Designed by Ian Hunt Design

Typeface: New Aster
Origination in Singapore under the supervision
of MRM Graphics

Contents

Measurements

Although care has been taken to ensure that metric measurements are true and accurate, they are only conversions from the imperial. Throughout the book instances will be found where an imperial measurement has slightly varying metric equivalents, usually within 0.5mm either way, because in each case the closest metric equivalent has been given. Care should be taken to use *either* imperial *or* metric measurements consistently throughout a project.

The sizes given in the cutting lists are the actual dimensions that the materials should be. For some man-made boards, manufacturers only specify dimensions in imperial or metric, not both. As some sizes do not translate from one to the other exactly, bear this in mind when you buy, and get the nearest size available in the measuring system you prefer.

METRIC CONVERSION TABLE

INCHES TO MILLIMETRES AND CENTIMETRES

mm = millimetres   cm = centimetres

INCHES	MM	CM	INCHES	CM	INCHES	CM
⅛	3	0.3	9	22.9	30	76.2
¼	6	0.6	10	25.4	31	78.7
⅜	9	1.0	11	27.9	32	81.3
½	12	1.3	12	30.5	33	83.8
⅝	15	1.6	13	33.0	34	86.4
¾	18	1.9	14	35.6	35	88.9
⅞	21	2.2	15	38.1	36	91.4
1	25	2.5	16	40.6	37	94.0
1¼	32	3.2	17	43.2	38	96.5
1½	38	3.8	18	45.7	39	99.1
1¾	44	4.4	19	48.3	40	101.6
2	51	5.1	20	50.8	41	104.1
2½	64	6.4	21	53.3	42	106.7
3	76	7.6	22	55.9	43	109.2
3½	89	8.9	23	58.4	44	111.8
4	102	10.2	24	61.0	45	114.3
4½	114	11.4	25	63.5	46	116.8
5	127	12.7	26	66.0	47	119.4
6	152	15.2	27	68.6	48	121.9
7	178	17.8	28	71.1	49	124.5
8	203	20.3	29	73.7	50	127.0

Introduction

Woodworking has many qualities to recommend it: the pleasure of exercising a manual skill and working with one's hands, the enjoyment of solving any problems that arise, and the added bonus of producing a useful object at the end. People who lead hectic lives often turn to hobbies such as woodworking to help reduce some of the stress and provide a sense of quiet satisfaction and achievement.

The concept of using a manual skill such as furniture making just for fun is a modern one, at least for the majority of the population. Originally, furniture was home-made because that was the only way to obtain it, and at its simplest would have consisted of a log to sit on and a roughly hewn board raised above the ground on stones or logs to make a table or bed. Later, villages and small towns would each have supported a number of craftsmen who provided the various artefacts that the people in the local community required. One of these would have been a carpenter who made the timber frames for houses, doors, gates, window frames and crude but serviceable furniture; only the larger towns would have had a specialist cabinet-maker.

All this has now changed: most affordable furniture is mass produced and there are very few craftsmen making bespoke pieces. However, there are also a growing number of woodworking enthusiasts, who make furniture simply because it is fun and gives satisfaction. This book is aimed at these weekend woodworkers, who make things for pleasure and to help furnish their homes. My hope is that people who already make their own furniture, as well as those who would like to do so, will find inspiration in the projects shown here, while the earlier chapters provide all the necessary information on tools, materials, construction methods and finishing to produce hand-crafted functional pieces that are enjoyable to make and use.

1 Tools

This chapter describes all the tools that were used in making the projects in this book. To some extent the list is a personal choice, comprising of the tools I feel most comfortable working with, and other woodworkers will produce similar results using a different selection. Fewer tools could still have done the job, but this might have taken longer, while more power tools would undoubtedly have speeded up the process. The choice comes down to individual preference and will inevitably be a compromise between speed, expense, accuracy and many other factors.

WORKBENCH

One of the most important workshop items, and one that it would be very difficult to manage without, is a firm working surface, preferably fitted with a vice. This can be a bench that is a permanent fixture, or one of the portable 'workmate' types.

FIG 1.1
A ³⁄₈in (10mm) portable drill, random orbital sander, and ¹⁄₄in (6mm) router.

POWER TOOLS

Whenever possible, I prefer to use hand tools because they are quieter, produce less dust and are probably safer. However, some jobs are definitely made easier and quicker with power tools and, in order to avoid unnecessary drudgery, a few power tools are very useful.

POWER SAW

A power saw complies with this description. The choice is between hand-held and bench-mounted versions, and there are many variations of both. My preference is for a bench-mounted band saw, which will rip and cross cut most materials with ease. One of its main strengths is that it is very versatile and will cut curves as well as straight edges.

Band saws are categorized by the width of board they can rip, as they are limited by the distance over the bed between the saw blade and the vertical part of the case which encloses the mechanism. So, for example, a 12in (305mm) saw will cut a maximum of 12in (305mm) from one edge of a board.

Another important dimension, which must be considered, is the maximum thickness of wood that can be cut, which is governed by the maximum gap between the bed and the upper blade guide.

Most band saws have either two or three internal wheels, upon which the saw blade is mounted in the form of a continuous loop. The two-wheel types tend to be more expensive and more versatile than those with three wheels, which are usually used for smaller, less demanding jobs. The bands come in a variety of widths and teeth configurations, but in general, straight cuts require a wide blade and curved cuts a narrow one.

Although all power saws are dangerous if not used properly, band saws are safer than bench-mounted circular saws. However, they are not as accurate, particularly when using a fence.

POWER DRILL

A power drill can be found in most households and is probably the first power tool that most of us own. They are characterized by the capacity of the fitted chucks, which are available from $\frac{1}{16}$in (2mm) for mini drills, to 1in (25mm) for large industrial tools. For the home woodworker, a $\frac{3}{8}$in (10mm) capacity will be big enough for most jobs. In general, the chuck size dictates the maximum twist drill-bit diameter that can be used. The exception to this is that some bits can be obtained with reduced shanks.

A modern drill will have many worthwhile features such as variable speeds, hammer action and screwdriving abilities, to mention just a few. They are usually far more accurate than hand-held drills, particularly if used with a vertical drill stand, and many useful accessories are available for sanding, buffing, grinding and shaping, including drum sanders, cutting bits, and wire brushes – the list is almost endless.

ROUTER

Routers are versatile power tools that have replaced many hand-held shaping and grooving planes. Because they are high revving, with speeds from 20,000 to 26,000rpm, they make a good quality, clean cut very quickly. They are graded according to the diameter of the collet that holds the cutter and are available in $\frac{1}{4}$–$\frac{1}{2}$in (6–12mm) sizes, which correspond to the shank sizes of the cutters, although some of the larger routers have collets that will allow the use of cutters with smaller diameters. Several accessories are usually supplied with a router, including a fence and various devices to allow the router to follow irregular shapes. A router can be used freehand or mounted on a table. Plunge routers are best for freehand use, but the plunging mechanism can be inconvenient when the router is mounted on a table.

There is a huge range of cutters to choose from which, for convenience, can be divided into two groups: those with bearings on the tips that are used to follow and shape an edge, and those that do not have bearings and can be used fully inserted into the wood for making grooves of different shapes and sizes.

SANDER

Random orbital sanders have been developed in recent years for the automobile industry for finishing car bodies. They are just as useful to the woodworker, as they will sand a surface without leaving any visible scratch marks and can be used to take off reasonably large amounts of wood quickly. On some types the sanding pads are fitted using Velcro, which is very convenient if frequent changing is envisaged. If you can only afford one sander, this is the one to get.

HAND SAWS

With the exception of the coping saw, all the hand saws I use are hard-point saws. This means that the teeth are hardened so that they stay sharp for a long time,

FIG 1.2
A drum sander and flap wheel attachments used for smoothing curves.

FIG 1.3
Tenon, panel and coping saws.

3

but when they do require sharpening this cannot easily be done by the home craftsman. Because of this, saws of this type will need to be replaced every couple of years, depending on how often they are used, but as they are reasonably priced this should not be too great a problem. Hard-point saws invariably have plastic handles, which are not as comfortable to use as the wooden handles on traditional saws.

Hand saws are normally categorized by the number of teeth to the inch. The smaller the teeth, the finer the saw cut.

PANEL SAW

A panel saw has a large blade approximately 20in (508mm) long, with about 10 teeth per inch. The teeth are shaped and set so that the saw can be used for both ripping and for cross cutting. For converting timber quickly or cutting man-made boards, it is very effective.

TENON SAW

A tenon saw is one of the most useful of the hand saws for making joints. It is made from thin steel, so has a thin kerf. To prevent the blade flexing when in use, it is supported with a strip of soft steel or brass along its back edge. The usual number of teeth is 14–16 per inch.

COPING SAW

Coping saws come in one size only. They are used for cutting curves in wood up to about 1in (25mm) thick, using a thin disposable blade which can be turned at different angles in the frame to facilitate cutting in awkward positions. The blade can be disconnected at one end and threaded through a pre-drilled hole to allow curves to be cut out from the centre of a board, leaving a frame of wood intact around the shape. Because the blade is extremely thin, it will cut acute curves.

CHISELS

My collection of bevel-edged chisels ranges from ¼in (6mm) to 1in (25mm) and covers most of my requirements. They are good quality tools, as it is imperative that chisels hold an edge for as long as possible and unfortunately, cheap chisels blunt quickly. Plastic handles are a good idea, because they will stand up to the occasional thump with a mallet which might break a wooden-handled chisel, unless it were reinforced.

PLANES

I use three or four metal planes for most of my furniture making.

JACK PLANE

The most versatile of these is the jack plane, which is used for the widest range of planing jobs, whether smoothing or jointing. It is about 14in (356mm) long and can be adjusted finely to take off thick or very thin shavings.

BLOCK PLANE

A block plane is a small plane used exclusively for planing end grain. It is useful for cleaning up the outside of boxes and carcasses made with dovetails on the corners, where it is used to trim the end grain of the pins and tails flush with the sides of the box.

REBATING PLANE

It is quite possible to make any rebate required using a router. However, I prefer to use a rebating plane, as it is less noisy and dusty. Whenever appropriate, as, for example, when

FIG 1.4
A set of bevel-edged chisels with high-impact plastic handles.

FIG 1.5
Jack, rebate, bull-nosed and block planes.

making open-ended rebates, it is a pleasure to use.

BULL-NOSED PLANE

A small, bull-nosed plane is used for trimming rebates or shoulders where you need to plane into a corner. This is because the blade is situated at the front of the plane body, with very little protruding in front of it. Because of its size, it is used with one hand only.

CLAMPS

It is an oft-repeated truism that you can never have too many clamps in your workshop.

SASH CRAMPS

I have four sash cramps of various sizes, which is enough for most jobs, but another couple would make gluing up some of the larger projects easier.

If a job requires more sash cramps than are available, loop a length of strong cord around the parts that require holding together and then twist a piece of wood into the loop, so that the string tightens and brings the parts together.

'G' CLAMPS

A selection of various sized 'G' clamps or similar devices is essential. I have four, which is adequate for most applications, but – as with the sash cramps – a few more would be welcome.

SHAPING TOOLS

These tools are used for smoothing curves and rounding off corners and edges.

SPOKESHAVE

I use a metal spokeshave, which is excellent for smoothing long, concave or convex curves or rounding corners and edges, if the cuts are not across the grain.

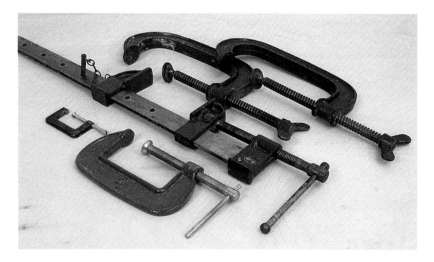

FIG 1.6
'G' clamps of various sizes, plus a sash cramp.

RASPS

Both round and flat surform rasps are good for rounding edges where the spokeshave has difficulty with the grain direction, as well as for removing the rough edges left after sawing curved shapes.

FILES

Files are used to smooth curved shapes after the initial shaping has been carried out with the rasps. I use flat, half-round and round, bastard and second-cut varieties.

MEASURING AND MARKING

Tools for measuring and marking accurately are as important as those that cut and shape.

ESSENTIALS

Pencils are a basic requirement. Choose those with medium to hard leads that hold a good point: cutting up to a very fine line is more accurate than using a wide, soft line.

A marking knife, marking gauge and mortise gauge are

FIG 1.7
Tools for shaping and smoothing curves.

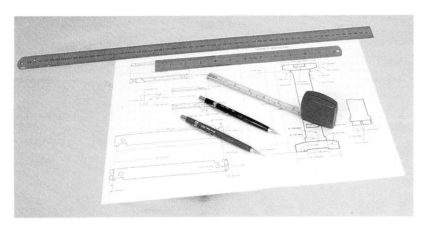

FIG 1.8
Rules and pencils.

essential items, as is a long steel ruler to use as a straight-edge. For measuring long lengths, pull-out steel tapes have replaced the folding boxwood rule that was traditionally used by carpenters, although I still have one that I use occasionally.

A good quality try square is also essential, and for preference I use one with a steel crosspiece, about 9in (229mm) long.

EXTRAS

Although not essential, a sliding bevel comes in handy for marking angles, particularly for sections to be cut out for dovetails, although it can be replaced by a dovetail template.

A pair of woodworkers' dividers are convenient for subdividing the width of a plank into several equal parts by 'walking' them across it.

MALLETS

Usually, when using a chisel, enough pressure can be applied by hand to cut effectively, but occasionally a few sharp raps with a mallet are required. Mallets come in a variety of weights and patterns. My preference is for a carver's type with a round head made from lignum vitae. Woodworkers' mallets with a rectangular head made from beech are just as effective, but not quite as nice to use.

HAMMERS

A medium-weight claw hammer is indispensable for driving in nails. When using panel pins to fix a plywood back into a carcass, or for any other application where a delicate touch is required, a lightweight pin hammer is worthwhile. For fixing the back on to a cabinet where the back will be out of sight, staples are an easy-to-use alternative to panel pins.

FIG 1.10
A medium-weight claw hammer, pin hammer and mallet.

DOWEL JIG

A jig combined with a power drill, this tool provides an accurate method of making dowel holes both quickly and reliably. A small amount of time will be spent in setting up, but once this has been done accurate joints are guaranteed.

Jigs that can be used for both ¼in (6mm) and ⅜in (9mm) dowelling are available. For some jigs it is possible to obtain extra-length rails that facilitate making the long rows of holes required for jointing boards edge to edge.

FIG 1.9
Marking tools.

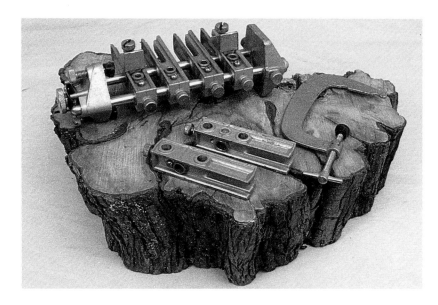

For a number of years I obtained reasonable results using a sharpening gauge with several different grades of stones. However, I now use a water-stone system with a leather-covered honing wheel; this has removed much of the drudgery from sharpening and gives excellent results.

Some woodworkers use a high-speed carborundum grinding wheel with good results, but these must be used judiciously. It is easy to overheat the cutting edge inadvertently, which will destroy the temper of the steel.

FIG 1.11
The Record dowelling jig.

SCREWDRIVERS

A selection of various-sized screwdrivers is important. They should have a ground square end and a comfortable grip. I find some of the modern plastic-handled screwdrivers unsatisfactory and use a set with boxwood handles, obtained some time ago, which are excellent.

From an old screwdriver, I have ground the blade to a point to serve as a bradawl.

SHARPENING SYSTEMS

It is not possible to achieve good woodworking without tools that are razor sharp. In this ideal state they require less effort to use, cut with greater accuracy and are inherently safer.

For plane irons and chisels, 'razor sharp' can be translated literally. After sharpening, test by shaving a small patch of hair from your forearm. To achieve edges that can pass this test, they must be ground to the correct angle and then honed. Although, with experience, it is possible to get the angle correct by hand and eye alone, if you do not have the time or inclination for the practice required, then a sharpening system of some kind is mandatory.

FIG 1.12
Screwdrivers with boxwood handles.

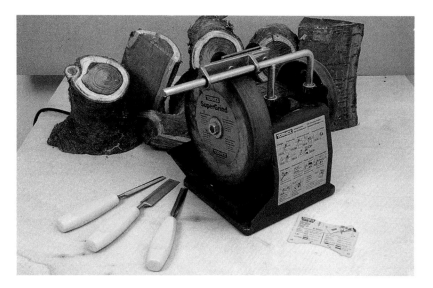

FIG 1.13
The Tormek sharpening system.

2 Materials

Most of the projects featured in this book are made from pine that was obtained from DIY outlets. These are not specialist timber dealers, but stores that sell timber as part of a wide range of products for the DIY market. For premium grade timber and for other specific requirements, stock will have to be bought from specialist dealers.

PINE

Buying from DIY outlets has many advantages: pine is readily available from them in a standard range of sizes, both sawn and planed; it is competitively priced; and many such stores harvest their timber from renewable forests. One of the disadvantages is that non-standard sizes are not available, so if you require a board that is, say, 1½in (38mm) actual rather than nominal thickness, you will have to buy a larger size and plane it to the correct thickness. In addition, DIY stores usually supply only one grade of pine, so if you need a plank with a large knot-free area you will have to pay extra for some premium-grade timber from a specialist dealer.

However, most of these disadvantages can be worked around, and for the home woodworker, DIY outlets provide a flexible and readily available source of good quality wood.

TYPES OF PINE

Trees are divided into two groups: deciduous and evergreen (including coniferous trees). The former shed their leaves in winter while the latter do not. Coniferous trees are also categorized as 'softwood'. This refers to a botanical classifi-

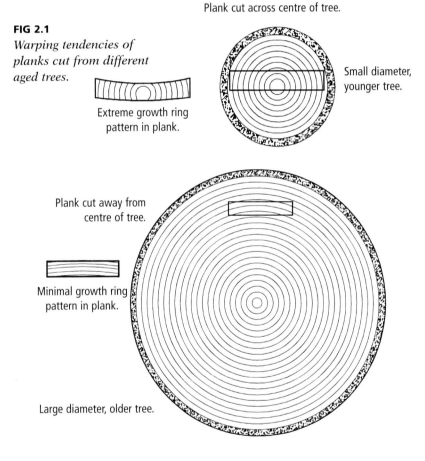

FIG 2.1
Warping tendencies of planks cut from different aged trees.

Extreme growth ring pattern in plank.

Plank cut across centre of tree.

Small diameter, younger tree.

Plank cut away from centre of tree.

Minimal growth ring pattern in plank.

Large diameter, older tree.

cation rather than the working properties of the timber, as some softwoods, for example yew, are harder than some deciduous 'hardwoods'.

Pine is a generic name which covers a variety of coniferous trees including different types of spruce, fir, pine and larch. Generally found in temperate northern forests, all these grow relatively fast, tall and straight and are sustainable, making

them ideal for the timber industry.

When choosing pine to make furniture, the type of wood you are offered will depend to some extent on where you are. In the UK it will probably be spruce, possibly from one of the Scandinavian countries, which is usually pale blonde in colour with slightly darker rings and dark-coloured knots. Some types of pine have more knot-free areas than others, while the age of the tree when it was felled also has a bearing on the quality of the timber.

Old trees are bigger trees. Most low-grade pine is from small diameter trees, about 8–10in (203–254mm). This gives rise to several problems. First, the branches of small trees are closely spaced down the trunk – approximately 12in (305mm) apart – so the knots are closely spaced. In big trees, where the branches are a long way apart, there are large areas of knot-free timber. Second, to saw a 6in (152mm) wide plank from an 8in (203mm) wide tree trunk, the cut must be across the centre of the tree, which means that it is more likely to warp (see Fig 2.1). The same size plank from a large tree has a less extreme growth ring pattern so it is less prone to warping.

ENVIRONMENTAL IMPACT

People today are concerned about the environment and this is one of the factors that is persuading the leading DIY retailers to obtain their timber from renewable forests that are managed for the paper and the building industries. Pine can be harvested from land that is not very useful for food production, so you can have a reasonably easy conscience about the environmental impact of your hobby.

SELECTION

Pine can be purchased with either a sawn finish or a planed surface. Sawn softwood will be at the size stated. However, when the wood is planed, about ⅛in (3mm) is taken off every surface, but the stated size is what it was *before* it was planed: this is called the 'nominal' size. So, for example, a piece of planed timber 6 x 1in (152 x 25mm) will have an actual size of approximately 5¾ x ¾in (146 x 18mm).

The sizes given in the cutting lists for the projects are the actual dimensions that the wood should be. However, for some man-made boards such as plywood or floorboards, some manufacturers only specify the dimensions in metric or imperial, not both. This leads to difficulties when compiling a cutting list as some sizes do not translate from one to the other exactly. For example, the nearest equivalent to ⁷⁄₁₆in thick plywood could be 10 or 11mm. When you purchase boards bear this in mind, and get the nearest size available, in the measuring system you prefer.

Although at DIY outlets the wood is very often shrink wrapped and standardized, it is still possible to sort through and select the planks to suit your purpose. In fact, it is probably easier to be selective in a DIY outlet than at a traditional timber merchant, some of whom may charge extra to let you sort through the stack. Be careful when selecting sawn wood, because it is not as easy to see faults as when inspecting planed timber.

Because you will need to be selective and discard wood with ugly faults, make an allowance of about 10% extra for waste when sorting the timber for a project.

FAULTS IN TIMBER

The different faults to be aware of are knots, resin pockets, warping, bending and twisting.

Knots

Knots are part of the inherent appeal of pine furniture and give the timber its character. However, some knots are desirable and some are not. Avoid very large, dark-coloured knots and those with cracks in them, as well as dead knots which might be loose in the knot hole (see Fig 2.2). Small, light brown knots are the ones to have (see Fig 2.3).

When selecting planks for a table or cabinet top, try not to use a piece that has a knot on the edge, because it will be harder than the surrounding area and therefore more difficult to work.

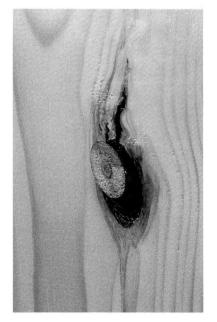

FIG 2.2
Undesirable: a dead knot, partially removed from its hole.

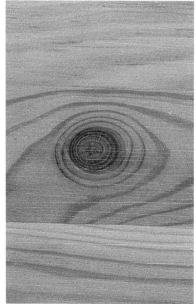

FIG 2.3
Desirable: a light-coloured, uncracked knot.

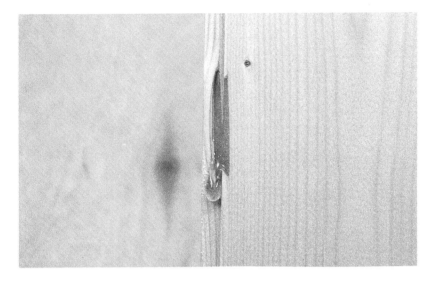

FIG 2.4
A resin pocket.

If a moulding of some kind is to be worked into such an edge, it will be very difficult to get it smooth. Similarly, when choosing wood to make a thin rail for a chair or table, do not pick a piece with a large knot in the middle as this will not only be weak but will also distort the shape.

If you have chosen a piece of wood with a dead knot which falls out after work has commenced, it can easily be glued back in. If the knot is cracked and breaks apart, as an emergency repair, it can be replaced with a plug made from a piece of similar-coloured wood.

Resin pockets

Resin pockets are found in nearly all types of pine and should be avoided wherever possible (see Fig 2.4). They consist of small hollows in the plank that contain an extremely sticky, semi-liquid resin, and are usually revealed when the wood is planed. If resin pockets appear in the middle of a piece of wood already being worked on and it is not possible to use another, the hollows can be cleaned out and filled, or cut out completely and another piece of wood shaped and inserted. However, neither solution is very satisfactory, and the best answer to the problem is to avoid resin pockets in the first place.

Warping, bending and twisting

These problems arise because a tree has a high moisture content when cut down and loses that moisture unevenly through the wood as it dries out. Wet wood shrinks as it dries, setting up stresses within the planks that in turn cause faults to appear. To alleviate this, the tree is cut into planks and dried either in the open air or in a kiln. The idea is to bring down the moisture content slowly to the same level as that of the place where the timber will eventually be used.

When planks are being dried, they are kept in stacks that hold them flat. When they are unstacked, brought into the DIY store and then sold, the moisture content of the wood may be slightly different to that of the surrounding air, causing the wood to either shrink or swell across the grain. This effect is not usually very marked until the wood is moved into a centrally heated house, when the width of a plank can change by as much as 10%: this figure will vary depending on the type of wood and its moisture content. It is therefore best to acclimatize the wood that is going to be used for indoor furniture by storing it inside the house for as long as possible before work is started.

A badly twisted piece of wood is very difficult to correct and should be avoided. A piece that is bent can sometimes be corrected by more extreme bending in the opposite direction, using weights or clamps for two or three days (see Fig 2.5). The best way of correcting a warped plank – where the wood bends away

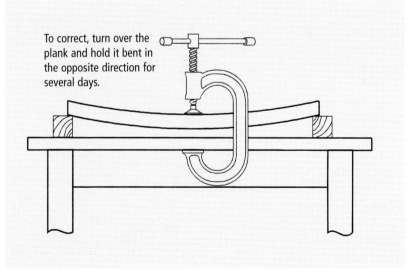

To correct, turn over the plank and hold it bent in the opposite direction for several days.

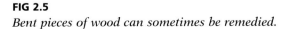

FIG 2.5
Bent pieces of wood can sometimes be remedied.

from the heartwood on the end grain – is to plane it to a smaller size (see Fig 2.6).

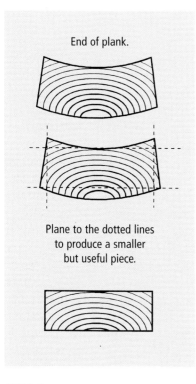

End of plank.

Plane to the dotted lines to produce a smaller but useful piece.

FIG 2.6
Correcting a warped piece of wood.

GRADES OF PINE

Pine is graded by assessing the amount of clear timber that is present in the boards, and the type of tree from which it came. If the wood is relatively free from knots, cracks, resin pockets and other faults, it will be of a high grade – referred to as 'appearance grade'. If it is not free from blemishes and flaws, it will be sold as 'building grade'. These two broad categories are subdivided still further by some timber merchants, according to the amount of defect-free timber and the straightness of the grain, although there is no consistency in the terms used for this. Generally, 'appearance grade' and 'clear timber' are of good quality in terms of appearance, while 'stress grades' refer to a lack of defects resulting in the timber being structurally sound and good for load bearing.

Unless otherwise stated, the planed timber sold in DIY stores will not be of the very highest grade. The sawn timber will be of the same or a slightly lower grade than the planed timber. Carefully select the planks you buy, and if you require clean planks for certain parts of a project either cut them from clear areas, which will waste some wood, or go to a specialist dealer who sells better grades of timber.

PREPARED BOARDS

Many DIY outlets sell pre-jointed pine boards ¾in (18mm) thick, in a variety of widths up to 24in (610mm). The boards are shrink wrapped and may warp slightly when opened and left in a warm room. To counter this, they should either be used immediately or stored flat with some weights on top.

AESTHETICS

When the wood has been selected for a particular project, there are some guidelines to follow which will enhance the appearance of the finished piece. When making a wide board from a number of planks, lay them out side by side so that you can arrive at the best arrangement. If there is one that has a different texture or colour, it should be swapped for one that matches the rest. If possible, the knots should be evenly distributed across the board in a random pattern.

The direction of the grain is also important. A panel looks best if the plank and grain direction is vertical rather than horizontal, as this makes it look longer and more elegant. Similarly, it is customary to have the plank and grain direction on a table top running parallel with the longer side.

Drawer fronts look very effective if the grain direction is vertical. However, it is often more convenient to have it running horizontally, as it is then possible to make the complete front from a single plank which will not require any joins. What should be avoided – unless it is a deliberate part of the design – is having the grain running horizontally on some drawer fronts and vertically on others.

Do not mix two types of pine with different knot patterns, textures or colours unless it is to achieve a design effect. For example, it can be effective to have the knobs on a drawer front made from a contrasting wood.

When selecting pieces of timber for a particular project, place the flawless pieces in the front where they will be seen and the rougher ones out of sight.

Most pine darkens with exposure to light. The stronger the light and/or the longer the time for which it is exposed, the darker it will become. If a picture or poster is pinned to the front of a pine cabinet and left for a couple of months, it will leave a lighter-coloured area when removed.

WORKING PROPERTIES

In general, pine is easily worked and can be planed to a fine, smooth finish. Most types are not suitable for use outdoors or for any application that might require excessive strength or durability. Pine can be sawn easily, but has a tendency to splinter on the back side of the saw cut unless a fine-toothed saw is used.

Because it is relatively soft, pine is very easily marked: you can apply enough force with a fingernail to dent it. Lay the wood on a smooth, clean surface before working on it, as any bumps or wood chips will cause a blemish on the underside if pressure is applied to the top.

MAN-MADE BOARDS

The only man-made boards used for the projects in this book are plywood and blockboard. There are many other types of board that will do a similar job, and you should make your choice based on fitness for purpose, expense, quality and ease of use.

PLYWOOD

Plywood is made from a number of slices of veneer which are laminated with glue to bond them together. Each layer of veneer is turned with the grain direction at 90° to that of the adjacent layers (see Fig 2.7). As a guide, good quality ply consists of a comparatively high number of thin slices of veneer, while low quality ply has a relatively small number of thick layers.

Plywood is available in a wide variety of sheet sizes, thicknesses and wood types, each intended for different applications. The thickness ranges from $\frac{1}{16}$in (2mm), intended for model-making, to at least 1in (25mm), which I have seen used for table tennis tops. Both hardwoods and softwoods are used; for furniture making, a softwood ply with a slice of high quality hardwood on the face is often a good choice.

Plywood has a number of advantages over large boards made from joining solid wood planks. Strength, flexibility and price are among its assets, but the principal benefit is stability, as it will not shrink or stretch under most conditions. The applications for which I find it most useful are drawer sides and bases, and the backs of cupboards.

BLOCKBOARD

Blockboard is made from a series of rectangular-shaped softwood strips glued edge to edge to form a board, which is then sandwiched between layers of veneer on the top and bottom faces (see Fig 2.8). It is available in large sheets in a limited range of thicknesses and is suitable for table tops, shelves and other applications.

ADHESIVES

All the projects in this book were made using white polyvinyl acetate (PVA) wood glue, which is relatively cheap and easy to use. Applied to a joint, it will hold after 20 minutes and be rock solid within 24 hours. It has a long shelf life, and will not stain the wood if a damp rag is used to wipe off the surplus before it dries. When completely dry, the glue join can be stronger than the surrounding wood.

To use PVA glue effectively, first make sure that the surfaces to be joined are clean. Spread the glue evenly on one of the surfaces, and use plenty so that it squeezes out when clamped.

SCREWS AND PINS

Where appropriate, screws and pins are used in constructing the projects. A small selection of screw sizes is adequate and most requirements will be covered by 1in (25mm), 1¼in (32mm), and 1½in (38mm) No 8 steel wood screws.

For fixing the backs into cupboards or the bottoms on to drawers, I usually use glue and panel pins or a stapler. The pins come in a variety of sizes, but ½in (13mm) and 1in (25mm) will suffice for most projects. If the pins are used in a position that can be seen, I punch the heads below the surface and fill in the resulting holes. If the pins are at the back of a cabinet that is intended to fit against a wall, they can be left unconcealed. In this situation, a stapler is probably a better tool for the job because it is quicker.

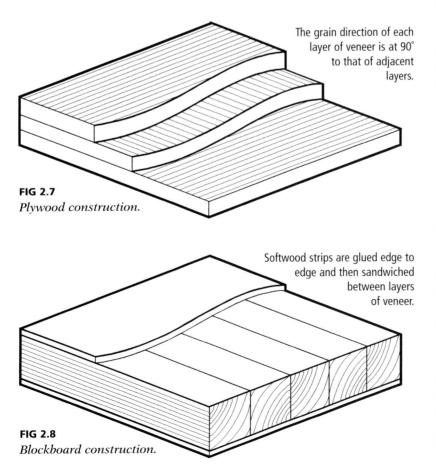

The grain direction of each layer of veneer is at 90° to that of adjacent layers.

FIG 2.7
Plywood construction.

Softwood strips are glued edge to edge and then sandwiched between layers of veneer.

FIG 2.8
Blockboard construction.

3 Construction methods

All the construction methods used to make the projects in this book are covered here. In many cases, more than one method would be appropriate for a particular piece, but I have chosen the most efficient in each case.

CARCASSING

Knowing how to make a carcass is fundamental to producing many pieces of furniture. In its simplest form, a carcass consists of four planks joined at the corners to make an open-ended box. Its strength depends on the material from which it is made and the method used to join the sides at the corners.

The applications are numerous, and include cupboards, chests and the drawers that go into them. The methods of joining the corners are also extremely varied: the carcass constructions in this book employ lapped dovetails, through dovetails, box joints, dowels and bare-faced housings.

Most carcasses used in furniture making require some method of strengthening or subdividing the basic unit. This usually consists of fitting shelves and partitions with housing joints; carcasses are also strengthened considerably when a back or base is added.

When a carcass has been glued and cramped, but before the glue is set, it must be tested to ensure that it is square. To do this, measure across both diagonals and compare the distances, if the figure is not the same, then the construction is not square. Sometimes if the difference is not very much it can be altered by repositioning the cramps. If this does not work, slacken off the cramps slightly. Cushion the corners with pieces of scrap wood to ensure they are not damaged, lay a sash cramp across the longest diagonal and tighten it until the diagonals measure the same. Once this is done tighten the original cramps again.

FIG 3.1
Test for 'squareness'.

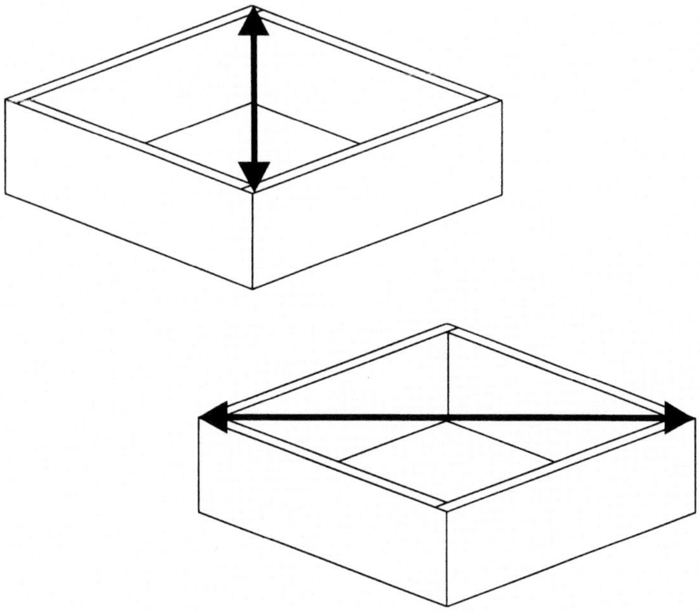

To test for squareness, measure each diagonal and adjust until both measurements are the same.

BOARD AND BATTEN

For many applications, including table tops and cupboard doors, you will need to make wide boards from a number of much narrower planks by jointing them edge to edge. To strengthen and hold these composite boards flat, one or more battens are fixed to the back at 90° to the boards (see Fig 3.2).

Because a wide board made of solid wood will shrink and stretch across the grain by a considerable amount, the battens are not glued into place. A common method for securing them is by screws that are fitted into slots in the batten rather than holes. This allows the boards to move slightly without splitting.

It is possible to acquire boards that are pre-jointed and shrinkwrapped ready to use. These certainly save time, and I use them whenever appropriate. However, the choice of thickness and wood quality is limited, so if you need a board of non-standard thickness and/or with fewer knots, pre-jointed board will not be suitable.

When edge jointing, pay attention to the grain direction as this will make a difference to the flatness of the completed board. Inspect the end grain of each piece and join them so that the side of the plank nearest the heartwood is alternately up and down. Then, even if each plank does warp slightly, the overall surface will be flat and any local troughs and valleys can be planed away.

If the planks to be jointed have been purchased planed on all four sides from a DIY store, it is a good idea to store them in the room where they will be used for a couple of weeks before working on them. In this way they can acclimatize to the

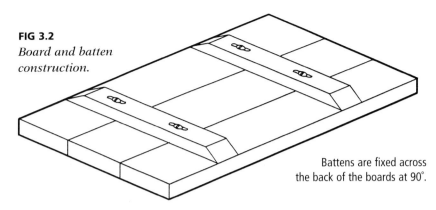

FIG 3.2
Board and batten construction.

Battens are fixed across the back of the boards at 90°.

conditions and any drastic shrinking or swelling should be over and done with by the time they are jointed together.

RAIL AND POST CONSTRUCTION

Rail and post is the descriptive title for the type of construction that requires upright legs with connecting rails. Typical applications of this are for chairs and tables, where the four legs are connected at the top by rails and sometimes also by stretchers half-way down the legs (see Fig 3.3).

Because such items will be subjected to a great deal of stress, the joints need to be

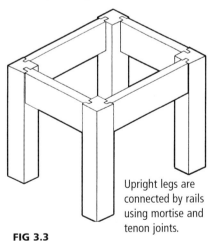

Upright legs are connected by rails using mortise and tenon joints.

FIG 3.3
Rail and post construction methods.

FIG 3.4
Frame construction.

strong and rigid. The classical joint for this purpose is the mortise and tenon, but the furniture industry often uses dowels.

FRAME AND PANEL CONSTRUCTION

Frames are used extensively in the construction of panelled doors and for the structural parts of cabinets, where the gap or gaps in the frame are filled with a panel made of glass, solid wood or plywood.

The construction method consists of a panel loosely fitted into grooves in a solid wood frame (see Fig 3.4). To allow for movement of the panel if the humidity changes, solid wood versions are never glued into place. If plywood is used, this is unlikely to be a problem.

DRAWER CONSTRUCTION

A drawer is simply a shallow box with a bottom fitted to it. The joints at the corners can be butted, rebated, box or dovetail, although typically they will be through dovetails at the back and lapped dovetails at the front.

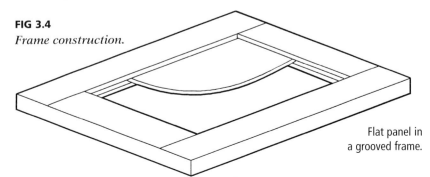

Flat panel in a grooved frame.

FITTING METHODS

A base-run drawer is the traditional fitting method. The drawer slides into and out of the carcass on the bottom edge of the drawer sides, and the tops of the drawer sides run against the upper rails when in the open position, preventing it from tipping forward.

Side-hung drawers are supported by two rails screwed to the inside of the carcass, which run in slots or grooves cut in the sides of the drawer. A carcass made for side-hung drawers does not require cross rails in the carcass between drawers that are stacked one above the other.

BASES

The base of a drawer is made either from planks butted together or from some form of plywood. The base of a very wide drawer is supported by a central bearer fitted to the front and back of the drawer.

The base can be fitted into slots cut in the four sides of the drawer, or supported on small square-sectioned pieces of wood or slip mouldings that are glued and pinned to the inside of the four sides.

FRONTS

There are several designs for drawer fronts that are widely used.

An inserted front slides into the carcass so that the front of it is approximately flush with the front of the carcass. To look good, this requires the drawer front to be an accurate fit in the drawer housing. A beading strip around the drawer front can be used to disguise any ugly gaps.

An overhanging front stands proud of the carcass and is usually larger than the drawer, so that it completely covers the drawer housing. This has the advantage of concealing any misfit between the drawer and the carcass.

A third method of attaching the front is to make the drawer as a complete open-topped box and then fit a false front to the existing front. This can be positioned very accurately, so that it fits perfectly into the carcass, before it is screwed into place. An easy method of accomplishing this is to put the drawer into the carcass and stick the false front in the required position with double-sided sticky tape, withdraw it from the cabinet and then screw the false front into place.

FIG 3.5
Drawer construction.

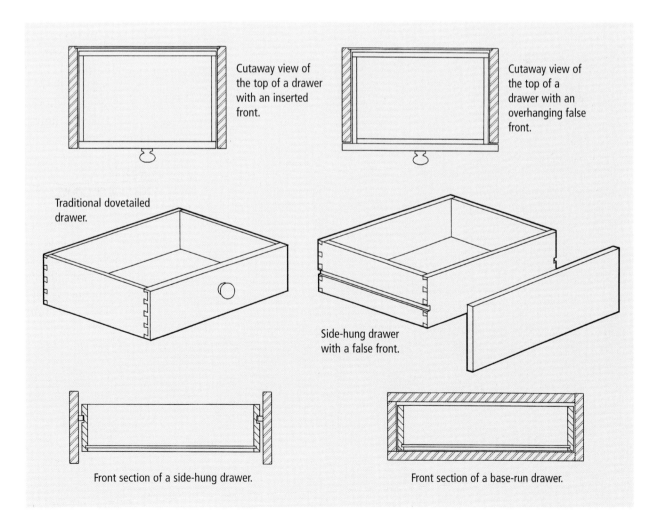

Cutaway view of the top of a drawer with an inserted front.

Cutaway view of the top of a drawer with an overhanging false front.

Traditional dovetailed drawer.

Side-hung drawer with a false front.

Front section of a side-hung drawer.

Front section of a base-run drawer.

4 Essential joints

This chapter covers all the joints used to make the projects in this book, each of which was selected as the best joint for the particular job. Detailed step-by-step instructions are provided alongside clear diagrams for each joint.

CARCASSING

BARE-FACED HOUSING JOINT

Used for joining the corners of any box structure and occasionally for fitting shelves, this joint is simple to make using

FIG 4.1
Making a bare-faced housing joint.

hand or power tools. When a carcass has to be made simply and quickly, and strength or decoration are not the overriding considerations, this is an acceptable method to use.

A rebating plane will cut the shoulders accurately, while the rebate housing can be cut with a tenon saw and chisel after first scoring it across the grain with a knife. A router with a straight bit

will cut both parts of the joint with equal ease, although it might take several passes for large joints in thick-section stock.

A bare-faced housing joint is slightly more complicated to make than a simple through housing joint and does not have any noticeable advantages for applications such as fixing shelves into a cabinet.

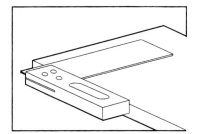

1 Mark the rebate on the first piece corresponding to half the thickness of the plank, and cut across the grain with a marking knife. On the adjacent corner, mark the housing for the rebate in the same way.

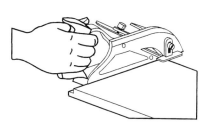

2 Use a plane to cut the rebates on the ends of the sides. It is easier to do this across the grain of the plank rather than on the end grain.

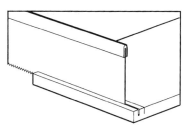

3 On the adjacent corner, cut the sides of the rebate housing with a tenon saw.

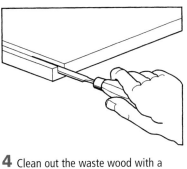

4 Clean out the waste wood with a bevel-edged chisel.

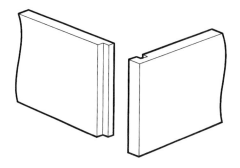

5 Test the joint for accuracy and adjust the fit if required. Do this on all four corners and then glue them together.

BOX JOINT

A box joint is often seen on the corners of small boxes or drawers, as it is very easily made using machinery and power tools. The side of the gluing area is approximately the same as for a dovetail, so if a modern adhesive is used, where the glue is stronger than the wood, the strength will be about the same for both joints. It is usual to make all the pins the same thickness, with the same distance between them.

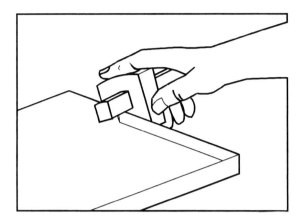

1 On the end of the plank where the joint is to be formed, use a marking gauge to scribe a line corresponding to the thickness of the plank.

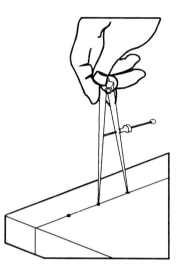

2 Decide how many pins are required and use a pair of dividers to mark the pin widths and the distances between them. Draw the lines that mark the sides of the pins parallel to the sides of the plank. Indicate the areas of waste wood.

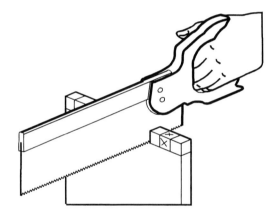

3 Cut the vertical sides of the pins with a tenon saw, ensuring that the saw kerf is on the waste wood side of the marked line.

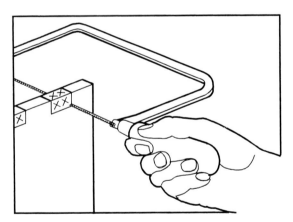

4 Remove the waste between the pins with a coping saw. Do not cut right up to the line: stop just short and remove the last small pieces by chopping with a bevel-edged chisel, held on the line and perpendicular to the surface.

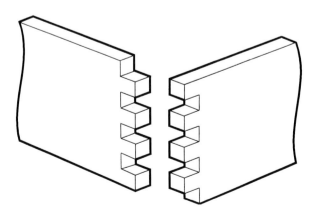

5 The joint should slot together quite easily without too much pressure. If it does not fit easily, make minor adjustments with a bevel-edged chisel.

FIG 4.2
Making a box joint.

THROUGH DOVETAIL

Through dovetails are the classical way to make corner joints and possibly the most aesthetically pleasing. They can be made by hand or by using a router and a dovetail jig. If the set-up time is discounted, the jig is quicker and probably more accurate. However, the problem with most jig-cut dovetails is that the gaps between the tails and the width of the tails is the same dimension. When cutting by hand, the tails can be made wider than the pins, which gives a pleasing hand-made appearance.

Making through dovetails by hand requires some practice, but the results can be well worth the effort. A typical application is for the corners of a drawer, where the back meets the sides.

FIG 4.3
Making a through dovetail.

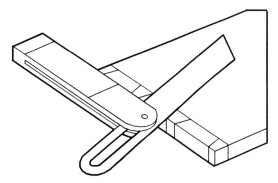

1 On the end of the plank where the joint is to be made, use a marking gauge to scribe a line corresponding to the thickness of the plank, then mark the angle for the slope of the tails with a sliding bevel. For softwood, the slope is usually 6:1.

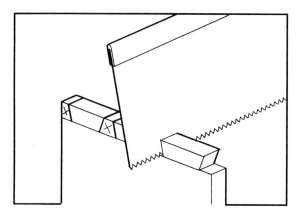

2 Scribe the line along the base of the waste area with a marking knife, and then cut the sides of the tails with a tenon saw.

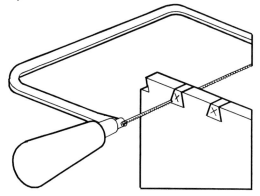

3 Cut away the waste between the pins with a coping saw, but do not cut right up to the line at this stage.

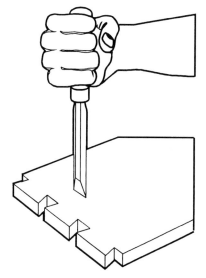

4 Remove the waste up to the line with a bevel-edged chisel. Place the chisel on the line and hold it perpendicular to the surface, then strike it with a mallet.

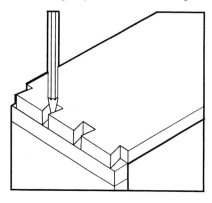

5 Use the tails to mark the position of the pins with a pencil. Project the lines along the faces of the plank parallel to the edges to mark the sides of the pins. Cut down the sides of the pins with a tenon saw and continue to form the rest of the pins using the same procedure as for the tails.

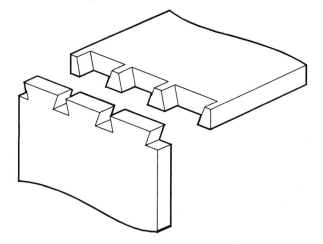

LAPPED DOVETAIL

Lapped dovetails are sometimes used for general cabinet work, but most commonly to join the front of a drawer to the sides. They are slightly more difficult to make than through dovetails and are employed where the joint on one face of the corner is to be concealed. It takes careful working methods to make an accurate joint.

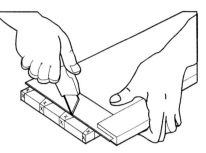

1 The tails are marked and cut in the same way as for through dovetails. The length of the tails should be between three-quarters and two-thirds of the thickness of the adjacent corner, which will contain the lapped part of the joint.

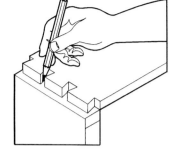

2 Use the tails as a template to mark the pins with a sharp pencil.

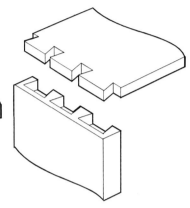

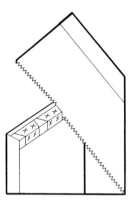

3 To form the sides of the pins, hold the tenon saw at an angle and cut in as far as possible without sawing into the lap.

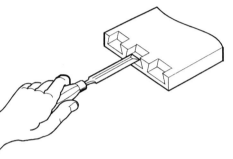

4 Remove the waste with a bevel-edged chisel and slot the two halves together to test for fit.

FIG 4.4
Making a lapped dovetail.

DOWELLED CORNER JOINT

Dowelled joints were originally invented for the mass-production furniture industry. Because making some joints in the traditional way is labour intensive and does not lend itself well to mass-production techniques, dowels are more cost effective.

By far the easiest way to make a dowelled joint is with a jig which, with care, will make an accurate, well-fitting joint. Effectively, it is a butt joint reinforced with hardwood pegs. The dowels can be made by cutting them from a length of straight-grained hardwood dowelling, or they can be purchased ready made. Make sure they are of an adequate length and sharpen the end with a pencil sharpener to make the joint easier to fit together.

Cut length.

Saw groove.

Sharpen end.

1 Dowels can be obtained ready-made, or formed from lengths of hardwood that are sold for the purpose.

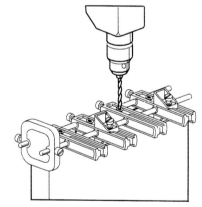

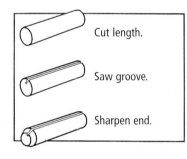

2 Using a dowelling jig ensures that the dowel holes are made easily and accurately. Mark the outside faces and top edges on the two corners to be joined. When drilling the holes, make sure that the bearing plates on the jig are up against these surfaces. This will ensure that the holes are lined up.

3 Insert the dowels in the holes and put the joint together. If it is satisfactory, take the joint apart, apply glue, fit it together and clamp until stuck. Clean up the outside of the joint with a plane.

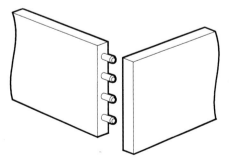

FIG 4.5
Making a dowelled corner joint.

HOUSING JOINTS

THROUGH HOUSING JOINT

Through housing joints are used mainly for fixing shelves and partitions into cabinets. When used for shelves, as in the projects in this book, they require a housing to be cut into the uprights. This can be done with hand or power tools.

Unless glued securely, the simpler versions of the through housing joint do not have much mechanical strength. If the joint is used for a long shelf, which carries a lot of weight but is not supported in the middle, the shelf can be pulled from its housing when it bends. In a bookcase or cupboard that requires strong shelving, fixing the shelves to the back with pins or glue will make all the difference.

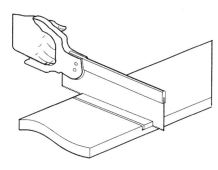

1 Cut the boards to size and plane the ends flat and square. With a try square, pencil and marking gauge, draw the position of the shelf housing. Use a marking knife to scribe the lines across the grain to prevent any splintering when the sides of the housing are sawn with a tenon saw.

FIG 4.6
Making a through housing joint.

2 Clean out the waste wood with a bevel-edged chisel. If it is a long housing, you will have to work from both sides of the board. Check the depth frequently with a steel rule.

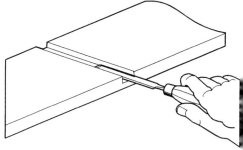

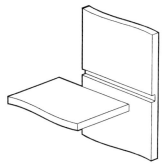

STOPPED HOUSING JOINT

A stopped housing joint is used to fit a shelf that is set back from the front edge of its cabinet. It is a little more complex to make than through housing, but the finished joint looks more professional.

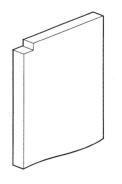

3 In the front corner of the shelf, cut a notch with a tenon saw to the same dimension as the depth of the housing.

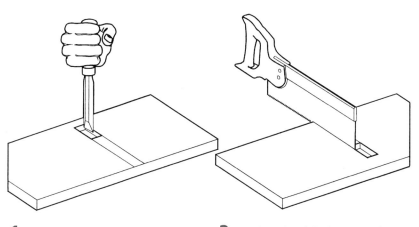

1 Present the shelf to the side of the cabinet and mark its position. Draw a pair of parallel lines with a try square to indicate where the housing is to be cut, and mark the distance of the rebate from the front edge. Scribe along the lines with a marking knife, and then use a bevel-edged chisel to excavate a rectangular hole that will provide enough space for the tip of the saw to move in.

FIG 4.7
Making a stopped housing joint.

2 Saw the sides of the housing with a tenon saw, then excavate the rest of the housing with a bevel-edged chisel.

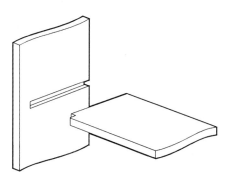

BOARD AND BATTEN

SIMPLE EDGE-TO-EDGE JOINT

You will need to know how to use this or one of the other methods of jointing edge to edge because of the difficulty of obtaining good quality wide boards.

If the planks that have been purchased are planed there is a good chance that only minor adjustments will be required to get a good fit. One of the difficulties in gluing this kind of joint is that the planks can slip out of alignment when under pressure from the clamps. Minor misalignments can be planed away when the glue has dried, but any major errors will ruin the board. Battens are often fitted to strengthen the board if it spans a wide, unsupported area.

FIG 4.8
Making a simple edge-to-edge joint with a batten.

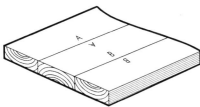

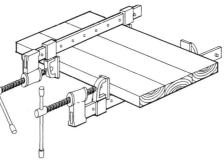

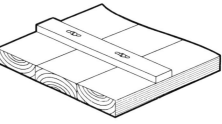

2 When gluing, apply the adhesive to one edge only and rub the two edges together to spread the glue. When clamping, alternate the positions of the clamps so that they are on both faces of the board.

1 To minimize warping, arrange the planks to be jointed so that the growth rings on the end grain are placed alternately. Indicate with identification letters which pairs of edges fit together. With the pairs of edges placed together AA, BB etc., plane both pairs of edges square and flat, so that they match when joined.

3 Battens are fixed to the back of the compound board to add strength and keep it flat. Screws are used in preference to glue; the boards will change size across the grain with changes in the humidity, and if glued securely the wood could not move and might split. The screws are fitted into slots rather than round holes in the batten to allow for this movement.

DOWELLED EDGE-TO-EDGE JOINT

The planks for this joint are prepared in the same way as for the simple edge-to-edge joints, and the dowels are added to assist in keeping the boards in line when they are clamped. As the dowels do not add to the gluing area, this joint is probably no stronger than the simple edge-to-edge joint.

A dowelled joint is simple to make with a jig, but can be very difficult to put together accurately without one, as it is not easy to get the holes to line up. If a jig is not available, a small and inexpensive aid to this is dowel pins. These fit into the first row of holes drilled, and are then pressed on the second edge to mark the position where the second row of holes is to be drilled.

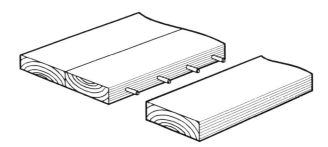

1 Prepare the edges of the boards in the same way as for the simple edge-to-edge joint. Using a dowelling jig, drill the dowel holes about 6in (152mm) apart. Prepare some suitable hardwood dowels. Apply glue to the edges of the planks, and push the dowels into the holes, then quickly push the planks together for clamping.

2 When clamping, alternate the position of the clamps so that they are on both faces of the board. Plane the faces flat when gluing up is finished.

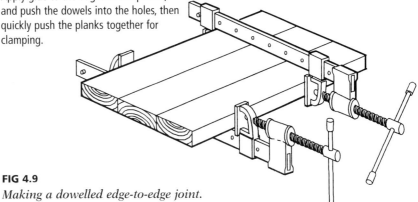

FIG 4.9
Making a dowelled edge-to-edge joint.

TONGUE AND GROOVE JOINT

If the size of boards required corresponds to the standard sizes available in your DIY store, planks that have the tongue and groove cut in them from stock are a useful and a quick way of making up wide boards. Standard sizes of ¾ x 5in (18 x 127mm) and ¾ x 6in (18 x 152mm) are widely available and usually sold for floorboarding. Some are also available at ⅜in (9mm) thick and are sold as cladding. The tongue is shorter than the depth of the groove so that the joint will not have a gap when the two parts are pushed together, as would be the case if the tongue were longer. Simply glue up and clamp lightly.

Cutting the tongue and groove with a router will make a good strong joint, but careful setting up is required – and there are better ways of jointing two planks (see above).

The tongue is shorter than the depth of the groove so that there will be no gap in the joint.

FIG 4.10
Tongue and groove joint.

RAIL AND POST CONSTRUCTION

MORTISE AND TENON JOINT

Mortise and tenon is a traditional joint that has been used for centuries and can be seen in medieval houses, usually employing pegs or tusks. The tenons are not usually very long: 4in (102mm) is the maximum length for furniture.

There are many variations of this joint for different applications. Tusked tenons are used when the furniture is knocked down (i.e., can be taken apart for storage) or sometimes for decoration; often they are reinforced with pegs for strength. A 'stub' or 'stopped' mortise and tenon is a variation in which the tenon does not penetrate right through the part that contains the mortise.

The mortise and tenon joint is one of the strongest ways of jointing two pieces in a T-joint, and is traditionally used for fixing the legs to the frame on tables and chairs that use rail and post construction methods.

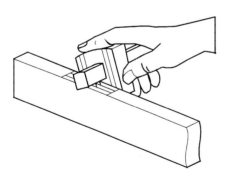 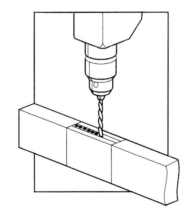 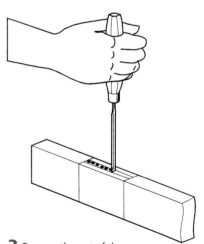

1 Use a try square to indicate where the mortise is to be cut. Set the mortise gauge to the required width, which is usually between one-third and one-quarter of the width of the wood, and scribe the lines.

2 Using a power drill fitted in a drill stand, remove as much of the waste wood as possible.

3 Remove the rest of the waste with a bevel-edged chisel, using a paring action. Hand pressure is usually sufficient, but if it is difficult, a few blows with a mallet will speed the job along.

FIG 4.11
Making a mortise for a mortise and tenon joint.

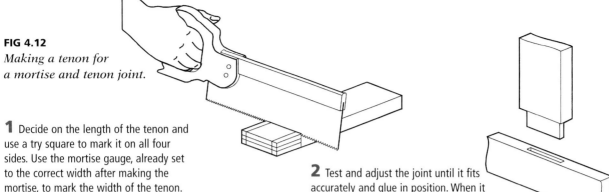

FIG 4.12
*Making a tenon for
a mortise and tenon joint.*

1 Decide on the length of the tenon and use a try square to mark it on all four sides. Use the mortise gauge, already set to the correct width after making the mortise, to mark the width of the tenon. Cut the tenon with an appropriate saw.

2 Test and adjust the joint until it fits accurately and glue in position. When it has set, plane the faces to clean them up.

MORTISE AND TENON JOINT WITH A HAUNCH

The usual application for a mortise and tenon joint with a haunch (sometimes called a 'shoulder' if it is sloped) is for the corner of a frame, where the haunch fits into the panel groove, to block it. However, it is also used for a mortise and tenon on the corner of a table or chair.

Allowing the tenons to meet in the centre of the joint and bevelling the ends will strengthen the joint.

The bevelled tenons meet in the centre of the joint to strengthen it.

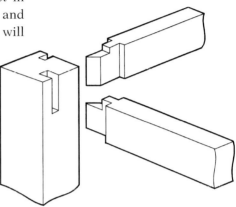

FIG 4.13
*Mortise and tenon joint
with a shoulder or haunch.*

TWIN MORTISE AND TENONS

Twin mortise and tenons are made where a single would be so wide that it might weaken the rail or frame into which the mortise is cut.

Twin mortise and tenons can provide a stronger joint.

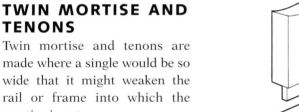

FIG 4.14
Twin mortise and tenons.

DOWELLED JOINT

Using a jig, a dowelled joint is an accurate, quickly made alternative to a mortise and tenon joint, although not quite as strong. To ensure that the post is not weakened when the dowel holes meet in the centre, it is a good idea to stagger the holes. This makes setting up the jig a slightly longer procedure, but enhances the strength of the joint. Apart from this minor variation, the method for making this dowelled joint is the same as for any other.

The dowel holes are staggered to avoid weakening the post.

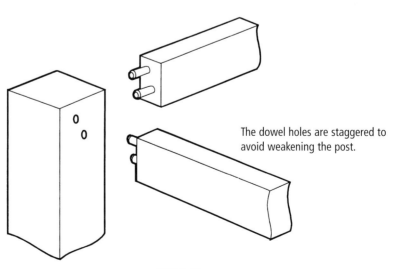

FIG 4.15
Dowelled joint for rail and post construction.

FRAMING

HALVING JOINT

Halving joints are used in frame construction where simplicity rather than optimum strength is the prime consideration. Wherever an easy method of uniting two rails or batons anywhere along their length is required, these are a practical option.

FIG 4.16
Making a halving joint.

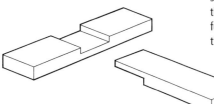

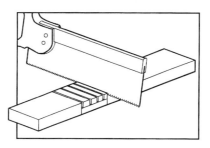

1 Lay one rail on top of the other at 90° and draw a line on both sides of it. Use a try square to make sure these lines are square, and then project them around all four sides. On the edge, use a marking gauge to find the centre and then scribe a line between the previously drawn lines. Cut down the vertical lines with a tenon saw at the edges of the housing as far as the centre line, and make a number of further cuts to make it easier to remove the waste.

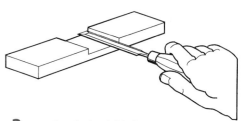

2 Use a bevel-edged chisel to remove the rest of the unwanted wood.

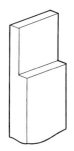

3 For the other part of the halving joint, mark the lines for the joint in the same way as before, and then remove the waste with a tenon saw.

DOVETAILED HALVING JOINT

This joint has more mechanical strength than the normal halving joint and is typically used in carcassing for the rail between the two sides of a chest of drawers. Because of the shape of the tail, it will strongly resist being pulled apart along the direction of the rail.

FIG 4.17
Making a dovetailed halving joint.

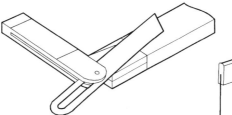

1 Mark a line on all four sides of the end of one of the pieces, corresponding to the width of the part to which it will be joined. With a marking gauge, scribe a centre line around the end where the joint is to be formed. Use a sliding bevel to mark the profile of the tail shape. The slope of the sides of the tail is 6:1.

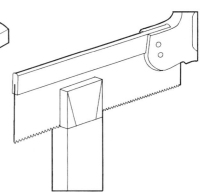

2 Using a tenon saw, cut along all the lines to form the tail.

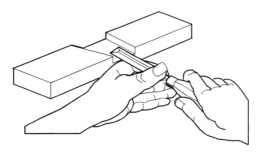

3 Mark the housing for the tail in the same way as the tail itself. Remove the waste with a bevel-edged chisel using a slicing action.

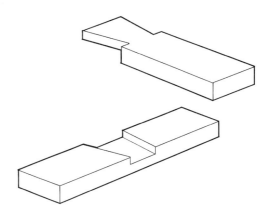

4 Check the joint for fit before gluing.

CORNER BRIDLE JOINT

A corner bridle joint is similar to a mortise and tenon and is used to join two rails at the corner. It has all the strength associated with this type of joint, which is derived from the large glued area. The tenon is generally one-third of the thickness of the wood being joined.

FIG 4.18
Making a corner bridle joint.

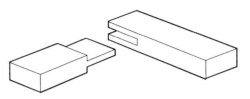

1 Lay one rail on top of the other at 90° and mark the width of the top rail on the lower one. Use a try square to extend this mark, and project it around all four sides. On the edges, use a mortise gauge to scribe lines between the drawn line and the end of the piece, for the width of the housing. Cut down the vertical sides along these lines with a tenon saw. Use a power drill fitted in a drill stand to remove the waste. Make a hole with a bit the same size as the width of the housing; this will remove the majority of the waste, but will leave a small amount in the corners to be removed with a bevel-edged chisel.

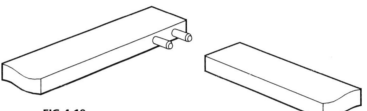

2 Mark the second half of the joint in exactly the same way as a tenon is made for a mortise and tenon joint. Try the joint for fit and adjust if necessary.

DOWELLED BUTT JOINT

With the use of a jig, a dowelled butt joint is a quick and easy alternative to one of the more traditional framing joints. The method is the same as for making any other dowelled joint.

FIG 4.19
Dowelled butt joint for the corner of a frame.

SCREWED JOINTS

Screws are a quick and effective way of making a joint in wood, and I use them extensively for construction work. Try to avoid screwing into end grain as this will not be very secure. If a number of large screws need to be inserted, make the job easier by lubricating them with candle wax.

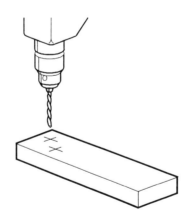

1 Drill a hole in the top piece slightly larger than the diameter of the screw.

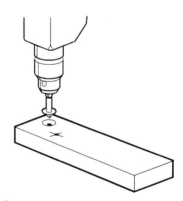

2 Countersink the hole for the screw head.

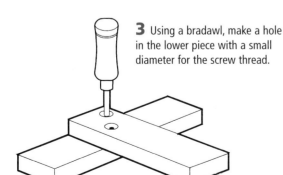

3 Using a bradawl, make a hole in the lower piece with a small diameter for the screw thread.

4 The screw should slide through the hole in the top piece and screw into the lower piece.

FIG 4.20
Joining wood with screws.

5 Surface preparation and finishing

One of the easiest finishes to apply and with which to achieve a hardwearing, professional finish is polyurethane varnish. As it is also an appropriate finish for pine furniture, nearly all the projects in this book have been finished in this way.

FILLING

Filler is used for correcting natural gaps and splits, and for filling joints that do not fit very well. When filling gaps in wood that will eventually have a clear finish, the filler must be the same colour as the wood.

Proprietary brands of filler paste are available in a wide range of colours to match various woods. Try them on a scrap piece of wood first, as they do not always match too well, many becoming darker as they cure. Some fillers might look the same when first applied, but if stained the areas of filler will show up as a different colour.

I often fill holes using a paste made by mixing PVA glue with fine sawdust from the vacuum bag on my sander. I push this into the holes using a flexible knife (see Fig 5.2), and sand it flat when it has dried. If the final finish is to be an opaque paint, a cellulose filler – the sort used for filling the cracks in walls before they are decorated – is adequate.

FIG 5.1
To prevent you inhaling dust that might be harmful, connect the sander to a dust extractor.

SANDING

Very often the smooth surface left after a piece of wood has been planed will require only a quick rub over with fine-grade glasspaper before it is ready for varnishing. However, in some cases this is not always adequate.

If the plane iron has small irregularities or is not set up correctly, it can leave slightly raised or indented marks, particularly if a wide board is being smoothed, and if there are irregularities in the surface of the wood, such as knots or twisted grain, areas can be torn out by the plane iron. In these circumstances, a random orbital sander is used for obtaining a fine finish.

The technique is to use progressively finer grades of sanding pad. If there are fairly deep hollows or tear marks, use a very coarse grade to take down the surface until these disappear. Follow this with medium- and then fine-grade abrasive. If there are no deep tear marks, the medium-grade abrasive will be adequate to start with. Change the pads when appropriate, and do not attempt to smooth away large blemishes with a fine grit pad, as it can take hours.

If the surface is finished by hand using a sanding block and glasspaper, the same principles of gradually reducing the abrasive grit size apply. For best results, always move the block in the direction of the grain.

GLASSPAPER GRADING

Abrasive papers are graded in grit sizes, either by a description of the grit size – coarse, medium, fine etc. – or by a number. A very coarse grade will have a number between 40 and 60, while a fine grade will be around 300. In other words, the lower the number, the coarser the grit.

A fine finish can only be obtained using a fine grade of glasspaper. Coarse paper that is worn down will not do, as it will leave occasional deep scratches.

SAFETY

Both powered and hand sanding produces large amounts of harmful dust. A random sander usually has a facility to connect it to a vacuum cleaner, which you should use if at all possible (see Fig 5.1). If you are sanding by hand or only using the small paper dustbag that comes with some powered sanders, a breathing mask should be worn.

VARNISHING

Polyurethane varnish is available in various colours or clear, the latter in at least three different textures: gloss, satin and matt.

Varnish should be applied in a dust-free atmosphere and in the direction of the wood grain, either using a brush or wiped on with a lint-free cloth pad. The first coat has the effect of raising the grain, so the entire piece must be rubbed over after the first application with fine-grade steel wool until it is smooth. Second and third coats are then applied, which in most cases will give the desired finish. However, for surfaces that are in a prominent position or receive a lot of wear, such as a table top, I sometimes apply a fourth coat.

On some projects I do not wait until all the construction is finished before varnishing, as it is sometimes easier to get to all the inaccessible corners if it is done as work progresses.

When using varnishes of any description, make sure you are in a warm, well-ventilated room. Because of the nature of the solvents used in their preparation, follow the manufacturer's instructions carefully.

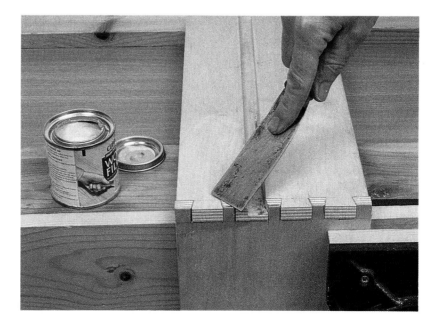

FIG 5.2
Applying filler with a flexible decorators' knife.

Projects

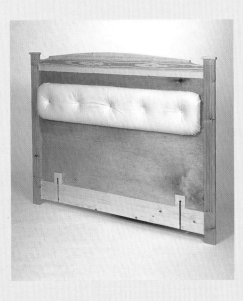

6 Kitchen stool

DEGREE OF DIFFICULTY: MEDIUM
TIME TO MAKE: 30 HOURS

This versatile stool is intended for use in the kitchen, so that the cook can sit down occasionally. The built-in step means it can be used to stand on to reach high shelves, when required.

CONSTRUCTION

STEP

1 I chose birch plywood to make the sides of the step because of its strength. Cut two rectangles from a small sheet, one for each side. Using a dinner plate as a template, draw the curved shape of the cut-out on the surfaces. Use a coping saw to cut out the curves and then smooth with a 6in (152mm) drum sander.

2 Cut the three cross rails that will connect the two sides to size and make the tenons for the bare-faced housing joints on the ends (see page 16). Form the corresponding housings in the two sides with a router, cleaning up in the corners with a bevel-edged chisel. Assemble without glue to check for fit.

3 Copper tubing is used for the pivot upon which the steps rotate. Carefully position the holes through which this passes in the sides. Make $\frac{1}{8}$in (3mm) pilot holes so that the large holes will be accurately placed, and then drill these using a $\frac{5}{8}$in

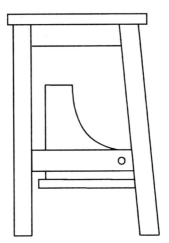

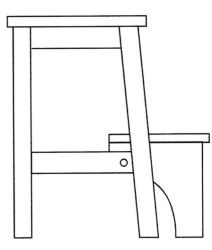

FIG 6.1
Side view with step in raised and lowered positions.

CUTTING LIST		
STEP		
Sides (2)	Birch plywood	9 x 9 x $\frac{3}{4}$in (229 x229 x 18mm)
Back rail (1)	Pine	10$\frac{5}{8}$ x 2$\frac{3}{4}$ x $\frac{3}{4}$in (270 x 70 x 18mm)
Front rails (2)	Pine	10$\frac{5}{8}$ x 2 x $\frac{3}{4}$in (270 x 51 x 18mm)
Corner brackets (4)	Pine	2 x 2 x $\frac{3}{4}$in (51 x 51 x 18mm)
Top (1)	Pre-jointed pine board	11$\frac{3}{8}$ x 9$\frac{1}{2}$ x $\frac{3}{4}$in (288 x 241 x 18mm)
Bearing blocks (2)	Hardwood	2 x 1$\frac{3}{4}$ x $\frac{1}{4}$in (51 x 44 x 6mm)
ALSO REQUIRED:		
Copper tubing (1)		13$\frac{1}{2}$ x $\frac{5}{8}$in (343 x 15mm) diameter
Nylon washers (4)		1$\frac{1}{2}$in (38mm) diameter, $\frac{1}{32}$in (1mm) thick
STOOL		
Legs (4)	Pine	19$\frac{3}{4}$ x 1$\frac{3}{4}$ x 1$\frac{1}{4}$in (502 x 44 x 31mm)
Top side rails (2)	Pine	10$\frac{1}{8}$ x 1$\frac{3}{4}$ x $\frac{3}{4}$in (258 x 44 x 18mm)
Lower side rails (2)	Pine	11$\frac{3}{8}$ x 1$\frac{3}{4}$ x $\frac{3}{4}$in (288 x 44 x 18mm)
Cross rails (3)	Pine	13$\frac{1}{8}$ x 1$\frac{3}{4}$ x $\frac{3}{4}$in (333 x 44 x 18mm)
Corner brackets (4)	Pine	2 x 2 x $\frac{3}{4}$in (51 x 51 x 18mm)
Top (1)	Pre-jointed pine board	14$\frac{1}{2}$ x 12$\frac{1}{2}$ x $\frac{3}{4}$in (368 x 318 x 18mm)
ALSO REQUIRED:		
L-shaped metal or plastic brackets (2)		
Pine plugs (2)		$\frac{5}{8}$in (15mm)

(15mm) bit. To ensure that the holes are vertical, use a drill stand.

4 Glue the rails to the sides and clamp for a couple of hours until the glue is set, then clean up the joints with a plane. Cut out the four triangular corner braces and fix in position with glue and screws.

5 Repair any gaps or defects with cellulose filler and then paint the step. The paint schemes for the step and the stool are the same. Prime the wood, then apply light blue undercoat followed by dark blue gloss. When the gloss is dry, rub the edges of the rails and legs gently with glasspaper to remove the top coat and allow the undercoat to show through, thereby highlighting the edges.

6 Cut the top piece for the step to size, varnish with clear matt polyurethane and then screw it to the steps.

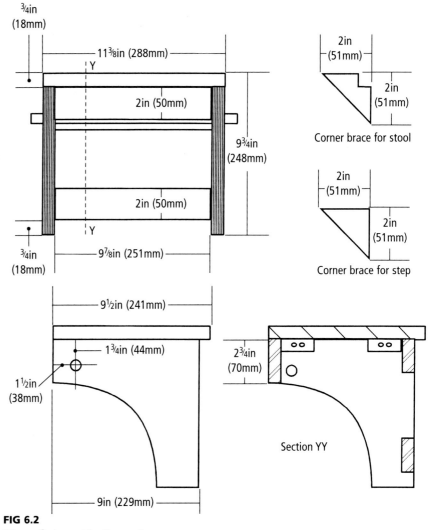

FIG 6.2
Plan of step with dimensions.

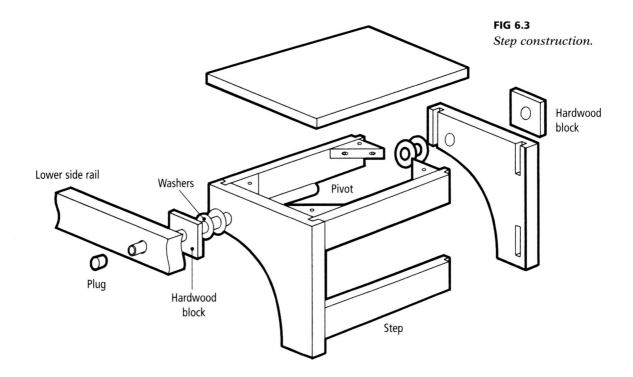

FIG 6.3
Step construction.

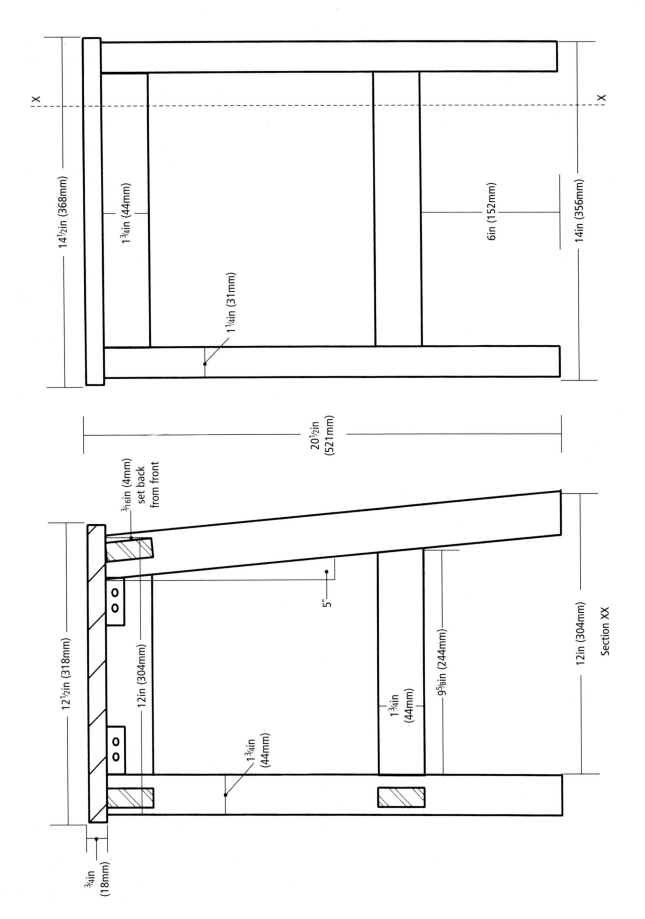

FIG 6.4
Plan of stool with dimensions.

14½in (368mm)

1¾in (44mm)

1¼in (31mm)

X

X

6in (152mm)

14in (356mm)

20½in (521mm)

3/16in (4mm)
set back
from front

12½in (318mm)

12in (304mm)

1¾in (44mm)

5°

1¾in (44mm)

9⅝in (244mm)

12in (304mm)

Section XX

¾in (18mm)

STOOL

1 Cut the four legs and the rails to size. Because they are sloped by 5° from the vertical, the two front legs are slightly longer than the back ones. There are two rails for each side and three long cross rails that join the two sides together.

2 The method of construction is to make and glue the two sides before joining them together with the longer cross rails. All the joints are mortise and tenons, with those at the tops of the legs having a haunch (see Fig 6.6; see also page 23). Because the two front legs slope by 5°, the tenons on the ends of the side rails which butt up to them have haunches that also slope by 5°.

To make the sloping tenons, set an angle of 5° on a sliding bevel and use to mark the haunches (see Fig 6.7), prior to cutting in the same way as for normal tenons. The tenons at the other end of the side rails and the ones on the longer cross rails are all made following the procedure on page 22.

3 Using the tenons as a guide for size, mark and cut the mortises in the legs. To make the job easier, drill some of the waste wood out first, and then use a bevel-edged chisel to chop out the rest. When drilling out the mortises for the side rails on the sloping front legs, the drill is held not at 90° to the leg, but at 5° off the vertical. In order to do this, make a jig with a 5° slope from scrap wood, to fit on to the base of your drill. With the legs held on this, it is much easier to drill the holes for the mortise at the required angle (see Fig 6.8).

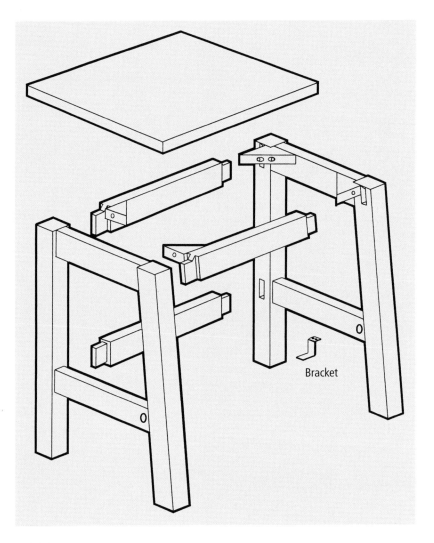

FIG 6.5
Stool construction.

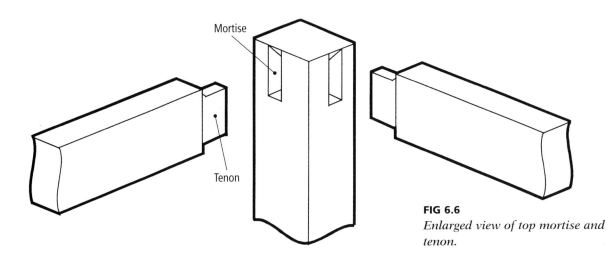

FIG 6.6
Enlarged view of top mortise and tenon.

FIG 6.7
Using a sliding bevel to mark the slope of the haunch for a mortise and tenon joint.

FIG 6.8
Drilling a sloping hole with a jig.

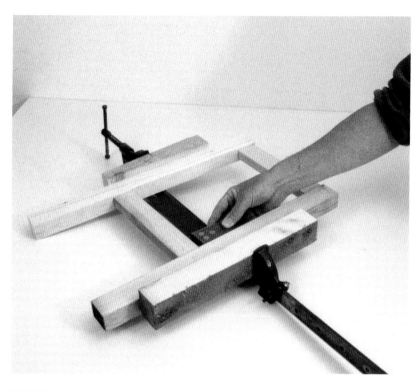

FIG 6.9
Ensuring that the stool sides are square when clamped.

4 Test each individual joint for accuracy, and then glue and clamp the two sides. Before the adhesive is dry, check that the structure is square (see Fig 6.9). When the adhesive is dry, lay one side over the other to check that they are exactly the same size, and make any necessary adjustments. Mark the ends of the sloping front legs at the correct angle using the sliding bevel and saw them off.

5 On the inside of the lower rails, where the holes for the pivots are to be drilled, glue on two hardwood blocks to strengthen them and help support the pivot. Now drill the pivot holes right through the rails and hardwood blocks. This will enable the step to be assembled into the stool once everything has been painted. When eventually the stool and step are assembled and the pivot is pushed into place, plugs of wood will be made to fit into the open ends of these holes to hold the pivot in place.

6 Assemble the two sides and the long cross rails and glue everything into place. To strengthen the assembly, cut out and fix the four corner braces to the inside of the top rails with glue and screws.

7 Cut the stool top to size and apply several coats of clear matt polyurethane varnish. Screw the top to the stool assembly. Paint the stool in the same way as the step.

ASSEMBLY AND FINISHING

1 Cut the copper tubing to the correct length. Place the step inside the stool and thread the tubing through the holes in the stool and the step, placing washers between the step and stool.

2 Make two softwood plugs to fit into the ⅝in (15mm) holes in the stool legs. I used a lathe, but a plug cutter in a drill would do the job equally well. Cut the

plugs to the correct length, so that they push up against the tubing at one end and are flush with the surface of the stool leg at the other. Glue into place.

When the glue is dry, finish with clear matt polyurethane varnish, so that they contrast with the blue paint. Swing the step into the stored position.

3 To prevent the step dragging on the ground in the stored position, a small metal bracket is screwed to the underside of the lower stool rail to support it. This is fabricated from two purchased L-shaped metal or plastic brackets. Using superglue, join the two pieces back to back to make a Z shape (see Fig 6.10).

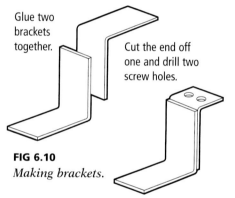

FIG 6.10
Making brackets.

Cut back one flange of the bracket so that it does not protrude beyond the thickness of the rail, drill new holes in it and screw it to the underside of the lower stool rail (see Fig 6.11).

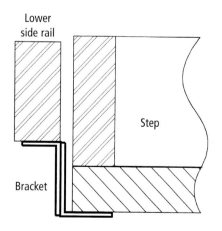

FIG 6.11
Section showing position of bracket to hold step in stored position.

7 Gate-leg table

DEGREE OF DIFFICULTY: ADVANCED
TIME TO MAKE: 45 HOURS

Gate-legged tables were first constructed in the seventeenth century and were probably developed slowly by a process of trial and error. Prior to this, tables had been large, heavy objects that were often constructed in the room they occupied, and were intended to be a permanent fixture. In contrast, the gate-leg table was designed to be pressed into service when required and tucked away against the wall when not.

Today, the design is ideal for a small kitchen or dining room where space is at a premium but a table is required for occasional casual meals. A drop-leaf table or one with a folding top would also be suitable, but I chose to make a gate-leg table as few other designs are as compact when folded yet so quick and easy to erect to full size.

CUTTING LIST

MAIN LEG ASSEMBLY

Main legs (2)	Pine	25 x 5 x 1⅛in (635 x 127 x 28mm)
Caps on top of legs (2)	Pine	9½ x 2 x 1¾ in (241 x 51 x 44mm)
Stands on bottom of legs (2)	Pine	10 x 2½ x 1¾in (254 x 64 x 44mm)
Lower rail (1)	Pine	26½ x 3 x 1⅛in (673 x 76 x 28mm)
Top rail (1)	Pine	25¾ x 3 x 1⅛in (654 x 76 x 28mm)
Brackets (2)	Pine	3⅛ x 3⅛ x 1⅛in (79 x 79 x 28mm)

GATES

Pivots (2)	Pine	20⁹⁄₁₆ x 1¼ x 1¼in (521 x 31 x 31mm)
Swinging legs (2)	Pine	27 x 1½ x 1¼in (686 x 38 x 31mm)
Top rails (2)	Pine	20 x 1¾ x ¾in (508 x 44 x 18mm)
Lower rails (2)	Pine	20 x 1¾ x ¾in (508 x 44 x 18mm)

TABLE TOP

Top planks A (2)	Pine	34 x 5 x 1in (864 x 127 x 25mm)
Top planks B (2)	Pine	34 x 5 x 1in (864 x 127 x 25mm)
Top planks C (2)	Pine	32½ x 5 x 1in (826 x 127 x 25mm)
Top planks D (2)	Pine	27 x 5 x 1in (686 x 127 x 25mm)
Top planks E (2)	Pine	14¼ x 2 x 1in (362 x 51 x 25mm)
Short battens (4)	Pine	8¼ x 1½ x 1in (210 x 38 x 25mm)
Long battens (2)	Pine	15½ x 1½ x 1in (394 x 38 x 25mm)
ALSO REQUIRED:		
Brass piano hinges (2)		36in (914mm)
Dowelling	Hardwood	¼in (6mm) for joints

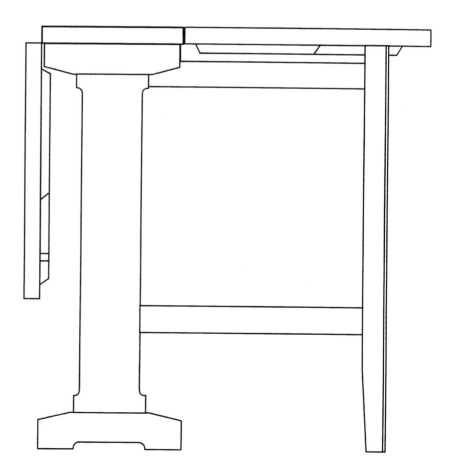

FIG 7.1
Side view with one flap raised.

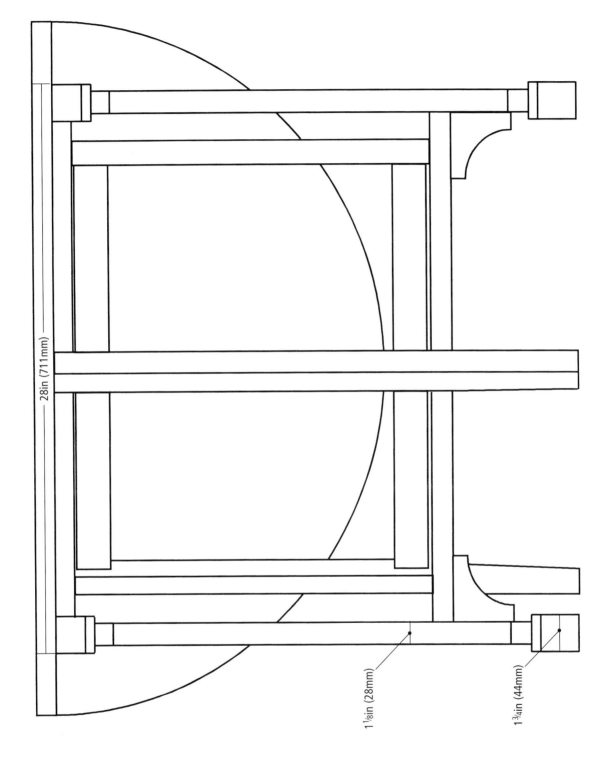

FIG 7.2
Front view with near flap raised, with dimensions.

CONSTRUCTION

Wherever possible I use prepared stock from a DIY outlet, but some of the thicknesses called for by this design are not available ready planed to the correct size. You will therefore need to buy sawn timber, cut it to the required size and plane it square. Planing down stock from larger sizes has the beneficial effect of eliminating any warping which may be present.

Sawn timber is more likely to contain cracks and defects, so select the pieces carefully. The structural parts of the table should be almost free of faults and knots. This is achieved by positioning the parts to be cut out on larger pieces of wood, carefully selecting areas where there are no defects.

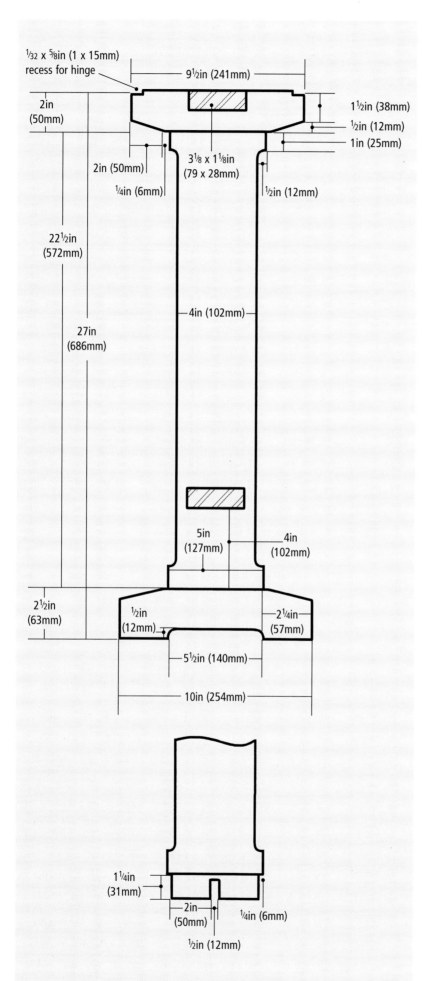

1/32 x 5/8in (1 x 15mm) recess for hinge

2in (50mm)

9½in (241mm)

1½in (38mm)
½in (12mm)
1in (25mm)

2in (50mm)

3⅛ x 1⅛in (79 x 28mm)

¼in (6mm)

½in (12mm)

22½in (572mm)

27in (686mm)

4in (102mm)

5in (127mm)

4in (102mm)

2½in (63mm)

½in (12mm)

2¼in (57mm)

5½in (140mm)

10in (254mm)

1¼in (31mm)

2in (50mm)

¼in (6mm)

½in (12mm)

MAIN LEGS

1 To prepare the timber saw it to approximately 1/16in (2mm) larger than the final size. Plane one of the wide sides flat, using a straight-edge laid across it to check for flatness as the planing progresses and adjusting as required. Plane one of the short edges smooth and use a try square to check that it is at 90° to the first side. Mark these two sides to indicate that they are square to each other. Plane the other short edge flat and, again, check it for flatness and also to ensure that the width – 5in (127mm) – is correct along its entire length. As the design requires a thickness of 1⅛in (27mm), set a marking gauge to this size and scribe along both edges, so that when the final wide side is planed flat the marks can be used as an aid to making the piece the correct thickness.

From these planed sections, cut the supports to the correct length. Cut twin tenons into both ends of the supports following the procedure on pages 22 and 23.

2 To make the caps and the stands at either end of the supports, again prepare the parts from sawn stock. Cut the pieces to width and length. Form the sloping shoulders with a saw and then plane them smooth. Form a recess on the underside of each stand. Mark the radius at the ends of this recess, using a 2p piece to get the correct curvature, and then cut out with a band saw. To smooth this small radius, use a ½in (12mm) round file and then some glasspaper wrapped around a ½in (12mm) dowel rod. Make the twin mortises in the caps and stands and test the joints for fit. Glue the caps to the supports.

FIG 7.3
Dimensions for main legs assembly.

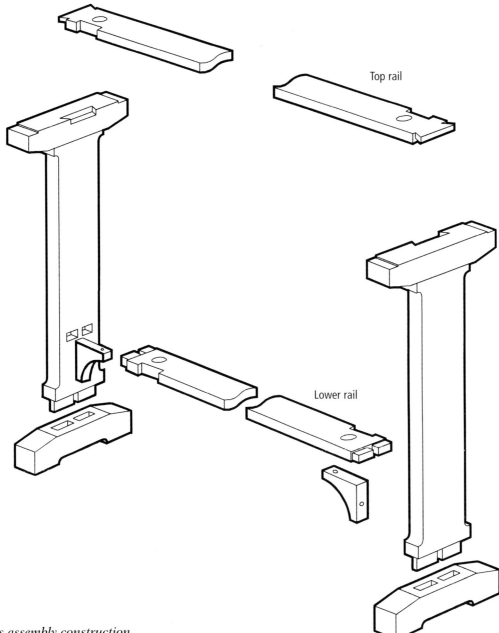

Top rail

Lower rail

FIG 7.4
Main legs assembly construction.

FIG 7.5
Cutting a recess for a screw in the top cap.

3 Cut screw slots in the top caps so that the table top can be secured to the legs. The slots will allow for expansion or shrinkage of the table top across the grain and prevent any movement splitting the wood. To make a screw slot, first cut a flat recess ½in (12mm) wide in the sloping shoulder of the top with a bevel-edged chisel (see Fig 7.5). This will both conceal the domed screw head and make a flat base for it. Make a screw slot about ½ x ¼in (13 x 6mm) by drilling three holes along its length and using a small, bevel-edged chisel and small, flat file to join the

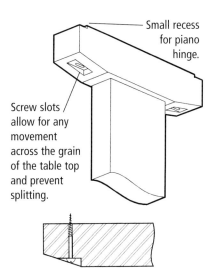

Small recess for piano hinge.

Screw slots allow for any movement across the grain of the table top and prevent splitting.

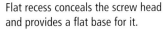

Flat recess conceals the screw head and provides a flat base for it.

FIG 7.6
Recesses and slots for screws in the main leg caps.

holes together (see Fig 7.6). On the top of the caps at the ends, cut small rebates that will allow clearance for the piano hinges when the table top is fitted on to the supports.

4 Shape the sides of the two supports by cutting out a decorative recess with rounded corners. The radii at the ends of these recesses are made in the same way as those on the undersides of the stands.

MAIN RAILS

1 Prepare the top and lower rails that connect the two main legs for width and length (see Fig 7.7). The top rail connects the caps that crown the supports and is slightly shorter than the lower rail, which joins into the supports.

2 Dovetailed halving joints are used for the top rail because of their mechanical strength. Also, when the base is assembled the gate upright pivots are held between the two main rails with pins that are formed on the ends and penetrate the rails. The top rail is lowered on to the legs to trap this pivot in place, and the dovetailed halving joint is ideal for this. Make the joints following the procedure on page 24.

3 Stub mortise and tenon joints are used to connect the lower rail to the legs because a through joint would show the ends of the tenons on the outside of the main legs, which look more attractive as unbroken lengths of wood. Make the joints in a similar way to those used for joining the caps to the supports.

Now glue the cap on to the supports. Assemble the supports and rails dry to check for fit and that the assembly is square, but do not glue at this stage.

4 In the top and lower rails, make holes to house the pivot pins for the gate legs. These should be 1in (25mm) in diameter and are made with a hole saw held in a drill in a vertical drill stand. First make a pilot hole, with a diameter of ¼in (6mm), right through the rail and then saw in from both sides with a hole saw (or large drill bit) until the centre of the hole can be removed.

5 Cut two notches in each rail so that the legs on the outer end of the gate can be tucked out of the way when the table is folded. The position of these can be found by assembling the table dry once the gates have been made and marking the position of the legs when folded.

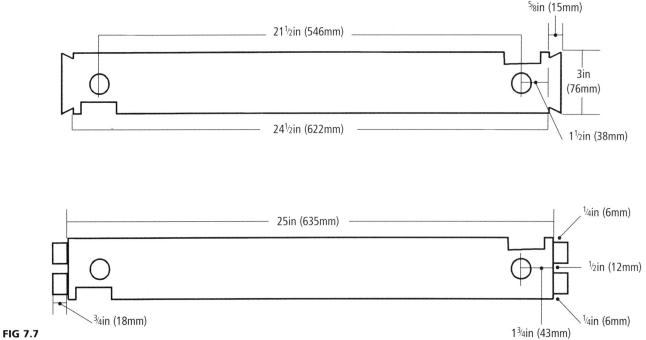

FIG 7.7
Dimensions for main rails.

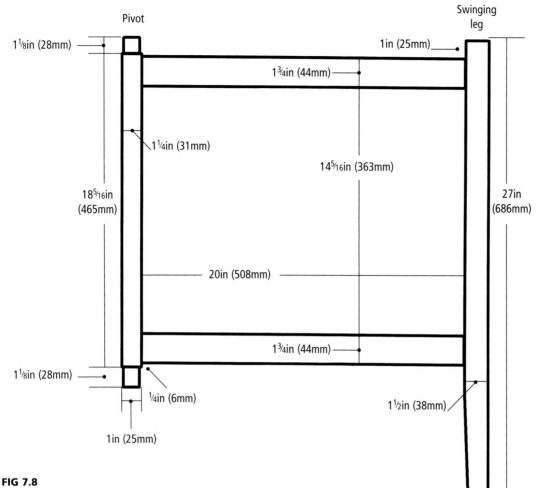

FIG 7.8
Dimensions for gates.

GATES

As the gates are identical, so is their method of construction. The instructions are for one gate, but you should make both of them at the same time.

1 The upright upon which the gate pivots has 1in (25mm) pins on both ends that act as bearings. These can be made in several different ways, but I used a lathe. An alternative method would be to use hardwood dowel with a diameter of ¾in (18mm) and glue it into holes drilled into the upright. Use ¾in (18mm) rather than 1in (25mm) dowel as it will leave some extra wood around the hole in the upright and make a stronger joint. The pivot holes in the main cross rails will also need to be ¾in (18mm) to accommodate the pins.

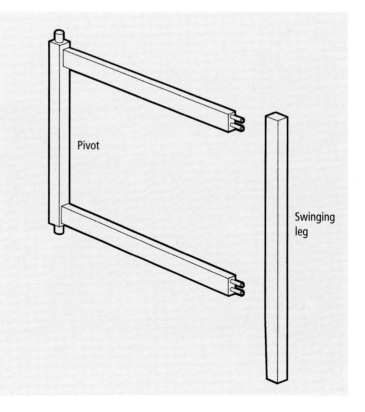

FIG 7.9
Gate construction.

2 If using a lathe, cut a piece of stock long enough to accommodate the pins plus some extra to allow for setting up on the lathe. Mark the positions of the pins and partially cut the shoulders with a saw to a depth of ⅛in (3mm) all round, so that when turning the pins, part of the shoulder is formed by the saw cuts – this simplifies the process.

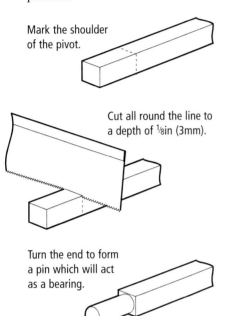

Mark the shoulder of the pivot.

Cut all round the line to a depth of ⅛in (3mm).

Turn the end to form a pin which will act as a bearing.

FIG 7.10
Cutting a pin on one end of gate upright to form a pivot.

3 Mount the wood on the lathe and remove the corners of the pins with a ½in (12mm) half-round gouge. Set a pair of callipers to the correct width and, using a ½in (12mm) flat-fronted scraping chisel, turn the ends until they are slightly larger than the correct dimensions. Now reduce them to the final size using coarse glasspaper held on a cork block. Make the pins slightly longer than required and trim them to size later when the assembled gate can be tried in its final position.

4 Prepare the leg for the outside of the gate that will support the table top flap, by forming a short taper at the foot with a saw and then planing it flat. Also prepare the top and lower rails. Make the joints for these parts using ¼in (6mm) dowels and a dowelling jig (see page 19 for general method). Assemble the gate dry and check for squareness (see Fig 7.11) and any twisting that may have occurred due to inaccuracies in making the joints. Adjust if necessary, then reassemble the gate with glue, check it for squareness and clamp until dry.

FIG 7.11
Checking the diagonals to ensure that the gate is square.

SUPPORTING BRACKETS

You now need to make two brackets, which are positioned under the lower rail joining the main legs to strengthen the structure. They will also support and act as a bearing plate for the gate pivots. A decorative radius is cut into them on the long side of the triangle, which reflects the smaller radii on the sides of the main legs and the base of the stands. I chose the size of this radius because it matches that of my 6in (150mm) drum sander, which is convenient for forming a smooth, curved finish on the brackets.

1 Mark out both brackets on a single piece of pine and cut the curve close to the marked radii using a bandsaw. Smooth the curve with a drum sander and cut the piece into two.

2 Drill and countersink two screw holes in each piece, as it is crucial that they are fixed into place as securely as possible. The brackets are secured to the legs with glue and screws, but are fixed to the cross rail with screws only as gluing might inhibit the movement of the gate pivot (see Fig 7.12). Fix the brackets in place when the rest of the leg assembly has been glued together.

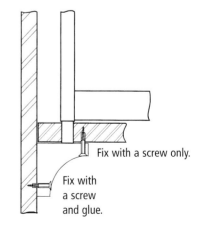

Fix with a screw only.

Fix with a screw and glue.

FIG 7.12
Section through pivot assembly.

ASSEMBLING LEGS AND GATES

Before assembling, clean off all pencil marks with glasspaper and bring all parts to a smooth finish. The leg assembly is put together dry so that the correct length can be found for the pins and the swinging legs, which were initially made oversize at both ends.

1 Using a flat, level area, put the structure together and then mark the length to which the pins must be cut. Take care to cut the length of the lower pin accurately: when assembled, the weight of the gate is taken on the end of the pin where it rests on the supporting bracket, and if the pin is not long enough its shoulder will rest on the lower rail that connects the two main supports, eventually wearing the rail and leaving it looking ugly. The pin should therefore be long enough to hold the shoulder $\frac{1}{16}$in (2mm) above the rail. Disassemble the structure, and cut the pins and gate legs to the correct length.

2 Before the assembly is glued together, varnish it with three coats of clear matt polyurethane varnish. Then glue and clamp the assembly together (see Fig 7.13).

FIG 7.13
The main support assembled with the gates.

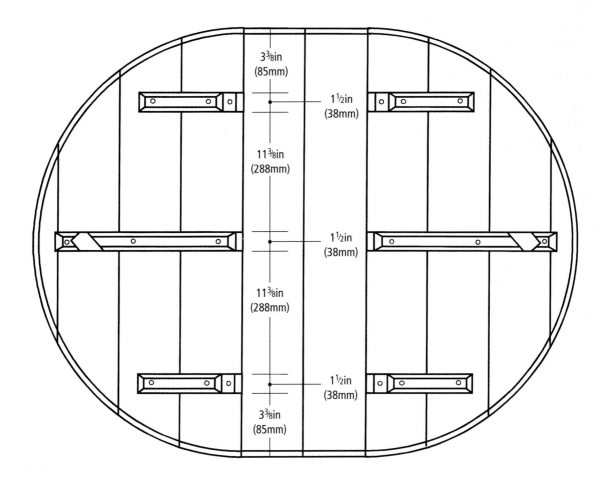

FIG 7.14
Table top showing position and dimension for battens.

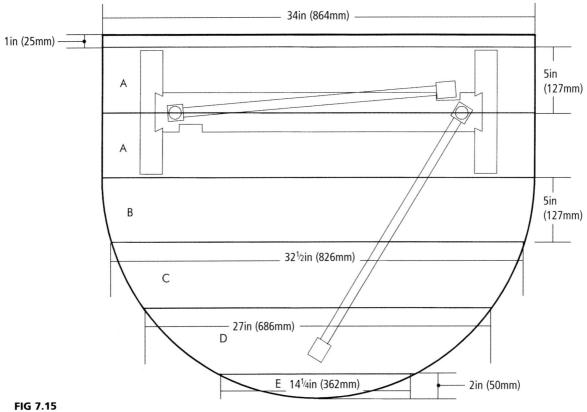

FIG 7.15
Part view of table top with dimensions.

TABLE TOP

The planks for the top are not a standard nominal size, so wood with a thicker section was chosen and planed down to size.

1 Cut the planks for the top to length and lay them down in position, with the growth rings on the end grain alternately up and down (see page 21). Cut the lengths slightly longer than required to leave enough room to form the rounded shape. Try to ensure that any faults or cracks are on the underside of the table top. Mark each plank to indicate its position in relation to the one next to it and which is the top side.

2 Start with the two planks that make up the centre section and, using a try square and plane, ensure that the edges are square to the face and that the planks butt together without showing a gap. Using a jig, make a series of holes for a dowelled edge-to-edge joint (see Fig 7.16; see also page 21). Fit the dowels into the holes but do not glue them, and test the joint for fit. Glue and clamp the joint (see Fig 7.17) and, when dry, plane the top and bottom surfaces.

3 To make the semicircular flaps you will need to make up a trammel bar from a scrap of wood to draw out the edge. This consists simply of a length of wood with a pin through one end and a pencil pushed through a hole in the other. The piece of wood should measure approximately 19 x ⅜ x 1in (483 x 9 x 25mm) and the distance between the pin point and the pencil point should be 17in (432mm).

4 Arrange the planks in the correct position to make one of the drop flaps and draw the semicircle for the edge of the table. This enables the dowels to

FIG 7.16
Drilling the dowel holes for the table top.

FIG 7.17
The centre section of the top, clamped together.

be positioned accurately and not too near the edge. Do not cut around the edge yet (the straight edges make clamping easier). Drill the dowel holes and then glue and clamp the planks together.

5 When the glue is dry, plane the top and bottom faces flat, using the plane diagonally across the boards as well as in the grain direction. If there is any tear out due to difficult grain, it may help to put the curling iron closer to the tip of the cutting iron and close the mouth of the plane by moving the frog forward a little (a large mouth opening is for removing a lot of wood fast, while a smaller gap is required for difficult grain). Redraw the table edge using the trammel and then cut out on a band saw. Make up the other flap in the same way.

6 Smooth the edges of all three sections of the top to take out any small humps and hollows left by the band saw. Use a plane on the flat edges of the centre section and a large file or rasp on the curved section, holding the rasp diagonally across the edge and as flat as possible. Stop frequently to assess progress visually and ensure that you are not putting in extra hollows.

7 Round off the edges, using a smoothing plane on the straight edges and a spokeshave on the curved edges. The method with both tools (see Fig 7.18) is to flatten off the corners in two stages to form half an octagonal cross section and then make a few cuts to eliminate the remaining corners. Remove any remaining flat spots with a couple of different grades of glasspaper held on a block.

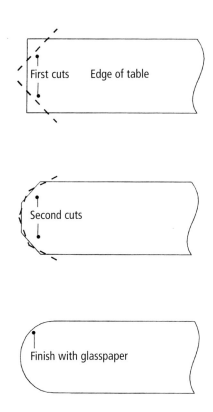

FIG 7.18
Rounding off the edge of the table.

BATTENS

It is very unlikely that the three sections of the top will remain absolutely flat. A slight curve is not a problem with the centre section, because it will be held flat by the screws which secure it to the caps on the main legs. However, if curving occurs in the flaps, this may be a problem. To avoid any distortion of the flaps they will need to be reinforced with battens, which are partially rebated into the underside of the top so that they are not too obtrusive (see Fig 7.20).

1 Cut the rebates for the battens with a router by running it along a straight edge clamped in the appropriate position. It takes a couple of passes to get the required depth of ³⁄₈in (9mm). Square off the ends of the rebates with a bevel-edged chisel. Cut the battens to size and length.

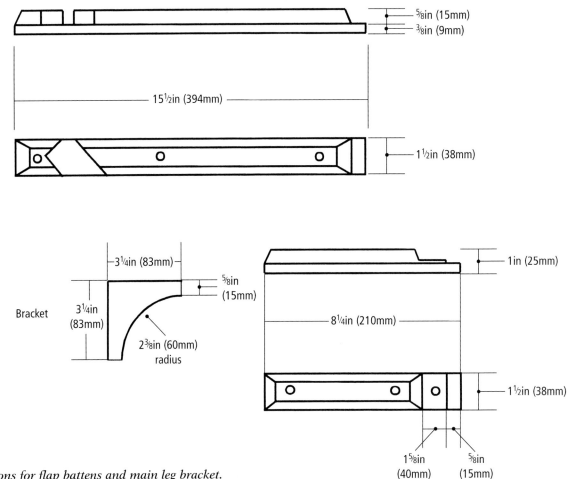

FIG 7.19
Dimensions for flap battens and main leg bracket.

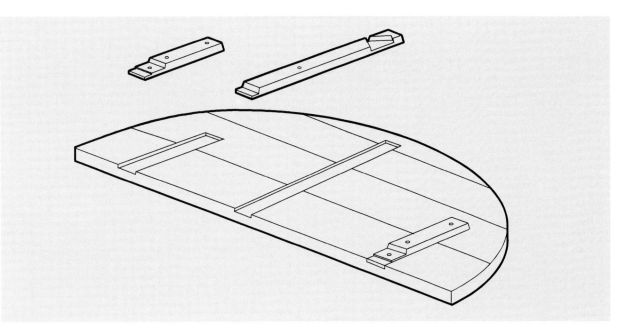

FIG 7.20
Fixing battens to underside of flap.

2 The battens are positioned so that when a gate leg swings it will bump up against the middle one. The middle batten acts as a stop to prevent the gate opening too far, and to facilitate this you will need to cut a recess in the centre batten to house the top of the swinging leg. To find the position of this recess, assemble the centre battens into the flap without screwing them. Place the central table section upside down on a convenient flat surface and butt the two flaps up to it, also upside down. On the centre section, place the main leg assembly in the same position as it will occupy when the table top is screwed to the legs. The table parts should all now be in their assembled positions, but inverted. Move out the swinging leg until it butts up against the central batten in the flap and mark the position for the recess. Using a tenon saw and bevel-edged chisel, cut the recess that will accommodate the top of the leg in the central batten.

Using a tenon saw, cut out a recess on each of the four short battens to give clearance for the caps on the two main supports

when the flaps are in the folded-down position.

3 Chamfer the parts of the batten that stand proud of the table using a smoothing plane. The angle of this chamfer is not critical, as its function is purely cosmetic. Drill and countersink oversize holes for the screws. (Making the holes oversize is an alternative to cutting slots to allow for wood movement: an oversize hole is large enough to allow the screw to move from side to side, but not so large that it will not support the screw head.) Screw the battens to the underside of the table top, but do not glue. If the top has already bowed slightly, clamp it to a flat surface such as the top of a bench before fixing the battens to it.

ASSEMBLY AND FINISHING

1 Unless you can obtain the exact size, cut down two 36in (914mm) piano hinges to 32in (813mm) and fit them into place, connecting the two flaps to the centre section to make a complete top.

2 Lay the top on the floor upside down and place the leg

assemblies on it in the inverted position. Check the action of the swinging legs to ensure that they locate in the correct place, both in the flaps and in the rails, and that the tops of the swinging legs clear the hinges. Make any adjustments necessary and then screw the leg assembly to the top.

3 Turn the assembled table the right way up and inspect the table top for flatness. If the flaps are not level with the centre section the swinging leg can be shortened, or if the legs are already too short, the area in the centre batten where the leg locates can be packed out with a thin piece of wood that fits the recess, to bring the flap up to the correct level.

4 Flatten the table top using a random orbital sander with a coarse-grit disk. Fill any blemishes or flaws with coloured filler and allow to dry. Go over the table top again using the sander with a medium-grit disk. Follow this with fine glasspaper on a cork block to produce the final finish. As heat resistance is required, complete the table top with three coats of clear matt polyurethane varnish.

8 Kitchen cupboard

DEGREE OF DIFFICULTY: EASY/MEDIUM
TIME TO MAKE: 35 HOURS

This small kitchen cupboard was designed to hang on a wall, with the base about 57in (1,450mm) from the floor and 17in (432mm) from the top of a work surface. I chose these heights to enable comfortable working practices, following those recommended in a table of anthropometric data specifying average dimensions for kitchen furniture (BS 3705: *Recommendations for the provision of space for kitchen equipment*, British Standards Institute, 1972).

With panelled doors and three drawers, the cupboard could be complex to make. To simplify the construction, wherever there is a choice of several suitable joints, the one that is easiest to make has been chosen.

CUTTING LIST

CARCASS

Top (1)	Pre-jointed pine board	29½ x 10 x ¾in (749 x 254 x 18mm)
Base (1)	Pre-jointed pine board	29½ x 10 x ¾in (749 x 254 x 18mm)
Sides (2)	Pre-jointed pine board	31 x 10 x ¾in (787 x 254 x 18mm)
Cupboard shelf (1)	Pre-jointed pine board	30 x 9 x ¾in (762 x 230 x 18mm)
Lower cupboard shelf (1)	Pre-jointed pine board	30 x 9¾ x ¾in (762 x 248 x 18mm)
Drawer partitions (2)	Pre-jointed pine board	5 x 9¾ x ¾in (127 x 248 x 18mm)
Front upright (1)	Pine	24¾ x 2 x ¾in (629 x 51 x 18mm)
Drawer guides (6)	Pine	8⅞ x 1½ x ⅜in (226 x 38 x 9mm)
Back (1)	Plywood	30 x 30 x ¼in (762 x 762 x 6mm)
ALSO REQUIRED:		
Fluted dowels, or length of hardwood dowelling (for joints)		

DRAWERS (FOR THREE DRAWERS)

Fronts (3)	Pre-jointed pine board	8⁹⁄₁₆ x 3¹¹⁄₁₆ x ¾in (217.5 x 94 x 18mm)
Sides (6)	Plywood	9¼ x 4¹⁄₁₆ x ⅜in (235 x 103 x 9mm)
Backs (3)	Plywood	8³⁄₁₆ x 4¹⁄₁₆ x ⅜in (208 x 103 x 9mm)
Cocked beading for sides (6)	Pine cladding	4⁷⁄₁₆ x ⅞ x ⅜in (113 x 21 x 9mm)
Cocked beading for top and bottom (6)	Pine cladding	9⁵⁄₁₆ x ⅞ x ⅜in (236.5 x 21 x 9mm)
Bases (3)	Plywood	8¼ x 8⅛ x ¼in (210 x 206 x 6mm)
ALSO REQUIRED:		
Pine knobs (3)		1½in (38mm) diameter

continued over

CUTTING LIST CONTINUED
DOORS (FOR BOTH DOORS)

Long frame sides (4)	Pine	24¼ x 2¼ x ¾in (616 x 57 x 18mm)
Short frame sides (4)	Pine	9⅞ x 2¼ x ¾in (251 x 57 x 18mm)
Short beading (4)	Pine	9⅞ x ½ x ⅜in (251 x 12 x 9mm)
Long beading (4)	Pine	19¾ x ½ x ⅜in (502 x 12 x 9mm)
Panels (2)	Pine cladding	20¼ x 10⅜ x ⅜in (514 x 263 x 9mm)
Knobs (2)	Pine	1½in (38mm) diameter
ALSO REQUIRED:		
Plastic corner brackets (2)		approx. 2 x 1 x 1in (50 x 25 x 25mm)
Brass butt hinges (4)		2in (51mm)
Brass door catches (2)		
Pine knobs (2)		1½in (38mm) diameter

CONSTRUCTION

CARCASS

1 Cut the top and two sides to length and width. Using a jig, make dowelled joints at the corners (see page 19 for general method) and assemble dry to check the fit. Glue the ready-made fluted hardwood dowels into the sides (see Fig 8.3), but at this stage do not glue all four boards together. The dowels will allow the carcass to be assembled dry several times to check the fit of various parts before finally being glued. If ready-made dowels are not available, make some from ¼in (6mm) dowel stock.

2 On all four boards, rebate the back inside edges where the plywood back will eventually be housed. The rebates on the two sides are stopped and should be made with a router, while those on the top and base are through rebates and should be cut with a rebating plane or a router. Clean up the corners of the stopped rebates with a small, bevel-edged chisel.

3 Cut the lower shelf that fits between the top of the drawers and the base of the cupboard to length and width. At each end, cut the notches that leave proud the part that will fit into the housing (the housings are cut

Section YY (excluding drawer sections)

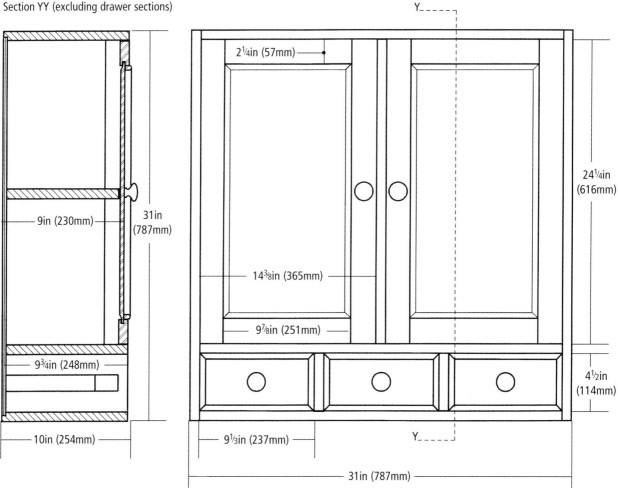

FIG 8.1
Front view and side section with dimensions.

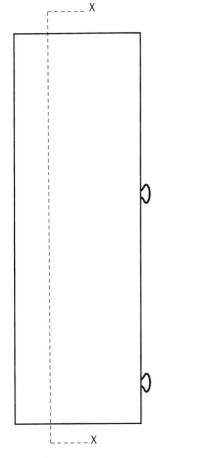

Section XX (excluding drawer sections)

29½in (749mm)

30in (762mm)

FIG 8.2
Front section of carcass with dimensions.

into the sides of the carcass later). On the underside of this shelf, mark the position of the recesses which will accommodate the two partitions that fit between the drawers. Mark the positions of the corresponding housings on the top side of the base of the carcass. Cut out these two partitions with the grain running from top to bottom, so that the edge that shows on the front of the cupboard has a similar grain direction to the edges of the sides. Cut out and fabricate the remaining cupboard shelf. Mark the housings on the two sides for the shelf to slot into.

4 Cut the housings for all the shelves and partitions using a router with a ¼in (6mm) flat-based cutter. It takes several passes to get the correct width for each housing joint. Clean out the corners at the stopped end with a ½in (12mm) bevel-edged chisel.

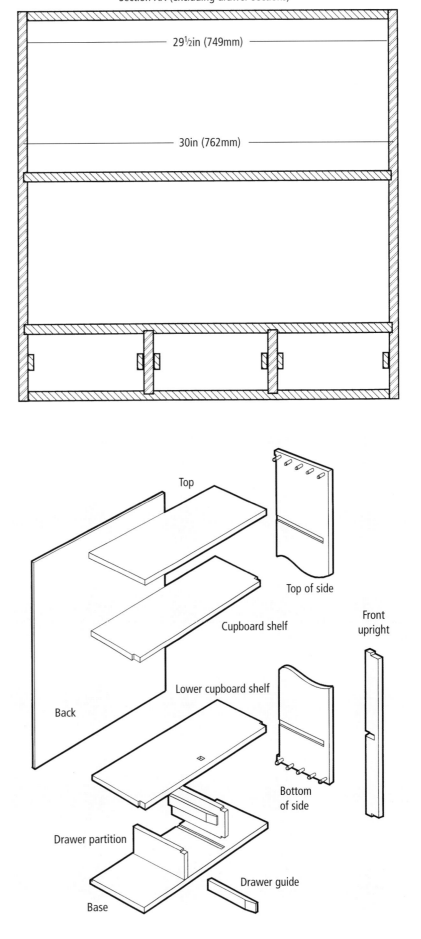

Top

Top of side

Cupboard shelf

Front upright

Back

Lower cupboard shelf

Bottom of side

Drawer partition

Drawer guide

Base

FIG 8.3
Carcass construction.

FIG 8.4
The assembly that houses the drawers.

for the upright that divides the front of the cupboard in two. Cut the tenons and notch into this upright. Cut the corresponding small slots that house this upright divider in the underside of the top and the top of the lower shelf with a router, and again use a ½in (12mm) bevel-edged chisel to clean out the corners.

ASSEMBLING THE CARCASS

1 Start assembling and gluing the carcass with the part that houses the drawers, then add the sides, followed by the upright in the middle of the cupboard and the top. Finally, slide the shelf into place. Clamp the whole

5 Assemble the carcass dry, starting with the drawer assembly (see Fig 8.4) and then adding the other parts to it, and mark the positions of the joints

FIG 8.5
The carcass before the back is fitted.

structure lightly with sash cramps, but before the glue has time to dry, check the diagonals for squareness and adjust if necessary. Remove any excess glue with a damp rag.

2 Cut the strips of pine for the drawer guides and chamfer the leading edge. These will fit into the drawer housings of the carcass and act as side rubbing strips to centre the drawers in the openings. Glue and pin the strips into the sides of the drawer housings. The front edge of each strip acts as a depth stop by butting up to the back of the beading around the drawer.

3 Cut the plywood back to size, but do not fit it at this stage: when the doors are made and fitted it helps if the inside of the carcass can be accessed through the back.

DRAWERS

1 Cut each of the drawer fronts to size with the grain running from top to bottom. (The fronts are smaller than the drawer openings in the carcass, because when finished they will have a cocked bead around the edge.)

2 Using a rebating plane, make a rebate $3/8$ x $3/8$in (9 x 9mm) on the inside of the two short edges of the drawer front to house the drawer sides. Make a smaller rebate $3/16$ x $3/16$in (5 x 5mm) along the lower inside edge of the drawer front where the plywood base will fit.

3 The drawer sides and back are made from plywood because the housing joint method of construction works well in this material. Plywood is readily available in the correct thickness and is not likely to warp even

though relatively thin, which can be a problem with solid wood.

Cut a strip of plywood to the correct width and long enough for two drawer sides and a back, with a small allowance for waste. Using a router and $3/16$in (5mm) bit, cut a groove along the lower inside edge where the plywood base will fit. Cut the plywood into the correct lengths for the sides and back and form a small notch in the front lower corner of the two sides. At the back edge of the two sides, use the router to make the housing for the drawer back. Cut out the drawer base and assemble the drawer to check that all the parts fit together snugly: do not glue the drawer at this stage. It will help to ensure that the drawer is square if the plywood base itself is exactly square.

Repeat steps 1–3 for the other two drawers.

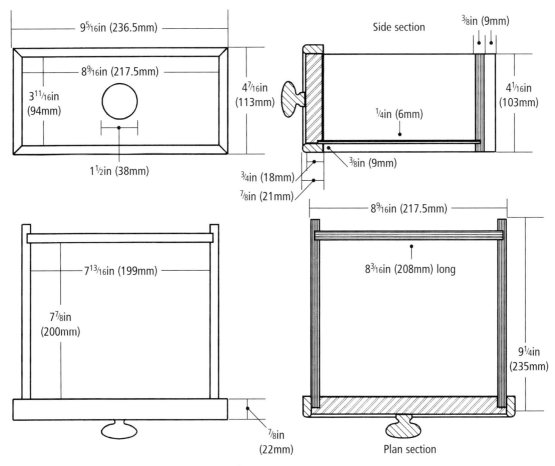

FIG 8.6
Plans and sections of drawer with dimensions.

55

ASSEMBLING THE DRAWERS

1 For each drawer, glue and pin the sides to the front and punch the pin heads below the surface (see Fig 8.7). Slide the base into the grooves and glue it to the front, but not the sides. Ease the back into place and glue to the sides only. Clamp across the back and check that the drawer is square.

FIG 8.7
Pinning the sides of the drawer to the front.

2 To make the cocked beading, cut a strip $\frac{7}{8}$in (21mm) wide and long enough to fit around a complete drawer front. Using a smoothing plane, round off the front edge and then cut the beading to size, with mitres on the corners. Check for fit, and then glue and pin the strips around the edges of the drawer front. So that the panel pins do not show, use a $\frac{1}{2}$in (12mm) gouge to lift a long shaving of wood without breaking it off. Put the point of the pin in the groove left by the gouge and hammer home. Punch the head of the pin below the surface. Glue the shaving back in place and hold it with a strip of tape while the glue

dries. When the glue is dry, clean up the surface with glasspaper.

3 Fix a knob to the centre of each drawer with screws and glue. Try the drawers in the carcass for fit and fix some end stops across the base at the back to ensure that the drawers do not go back too far into the spaces.

DOORS

1 For each door, cut the frame sides to size. The corners of the frame are joined together using dowelled butt joints (see page 25). Using a dowelling jig, drill holes in all four corners for the dowelling pegs and insert them so that the frame can be assembled dry to check for fit, size and squareness, and also to see that it lies flat without twisting.

2 Disassemble the frame and cut the grooves that will house the central panel, using a router with a $\frac{1}{4}$in (6mm) bit. Make the grooves in the cross members from end to end, but in the upright pieces stop them at the dowel holes at both ends. Glue the dowels into the cross pieces only, and test for accuracy.

3 To make each door panel, cut slightly oversize and join together a number of tongue and groove pine-cladding planks. Mark the final size of the panel on the front in pencil, ensuring that it is as square as possible before cutting it out. So that the edges will fit into the grooves in the frame, use a smoothing plane to chamfer them on the back of the panel so that the chamfers will not be seen when the doors are closed. Cladding planks are usually put up with the flatter side to the wall, but here the flatter side is on the front of the door, so that the decorative groove does not show on the front of the cupboard door.

ASSEMBLING THE DOORS

1 Varnish the edges of the panel before assembling each door, to help prevent the wood shrinking or expanding with changes in humidity. Assemble and glue the corners of the frame, with the panel loose and unglued in the centre (see Fig 8.8) – as it is a wide panel, it might change size and split if glued firmly in place. Test the door for fit in the carcass.

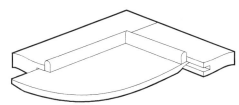

FIG 8.8
Detail of panel fitted in frame.

2 Prepare the lengths of beading in the same way as for the drawer front, except that this time they are not cut as wide. Fix the beading with pins and glue around the inside edge of the frame, not on to the panel.

ASSEMBLING AND FINISHING

1 Fix in the cupboard back with pins and glue. Fit the plastic corner brackets to the inside of the cupboard to provide support when it is fixed to the wall.

2 Brass butt hinges are used to hang the doors as they are a good choice for any environment that might get damp from steam. Fit small brass catches on the underside of the central shelf. Fix pine knobs to the doors to match those on the drawers.

3 Finish the entire cupboard with clear matt polyurethane varnish.

9 Kitchen work trolley

DEGREE OF DIFFICULTY: MEDIUM
TIME TO MAKE: 55 HOURS

This versatile, mobile kitchen 'island' is ideal for vegetable preparation. It has a thick 'butcher's block' work surface, with plenty of space underneath for frequently used accessories, and a wide drawer. The entire trolley will glide smoothly around the kitchen on castors, which lock securely when it is in use for food preparation. There is also a sliding extension to the work surface which pulls out from the side of the trolley.

The top is made from small blocks of pine which are arranged so that the top surface is the end grain of the blocks. As well as being very attractive, this is an ideal surface for chopping vegetables as it is durable and will not blunt knives.

CUTTING LIST

CARCASS

Large blocks for top (56)	Pine	4 x 2 x 2in (102 x 51 x 51mm)
Small blocks for top (14)	Pine	2 x 2 x 2in (51 x 51 x 51mm)
Legs A (4)	Pine	28 x 2 x 2in (711 x 51 x 51mm)
Deep back rail B (1)	Pre-jointed pine board	$21\frac{3}{8}$ x $6\frac{1}{2}$ x $\frac{3}{4}$in (543 x 165 x 18mm)
Shallow side rail C (1)	Pre-jointed pine board	$12\frac{1}{4}$ x $5\frac{1}{4}$ x $\frac{3}{4}$in (311 x 133 x 18mm)
Deep side rail D (1)	Pre-jointed pine board	$12\frac{1}{4}$ x $6\frac{1}{2}$ x $\frac{3}{4}$in (311 x 165 x 18mm)
Side top rail E (1)	Pine	$12\frac{1}{4}$ x 2 x $\frac{3}{4}$in (311 x 51 x 18mm)
Back top rail F (1)	Pine	$22\frac{3}{8}$ x 2 x $\frac{3}{4}$in (568 x 51 x 18mm)
Front top rail G (1)	Pine	$21\frac{3}{8}$ x 2 x $\frac{3}{4}$in (543 x 51 x 18mm)
Sliding shelf support top rail H (1)	Pine	$22\frac{3}{8}$ x 1 x 1in (568 x 25 x 25mm)
Sliding shelf side supports I (2)	Pine	$21\frac{3}{8}$ x 1 x $\frac{9}{16}$in (543 x 25 x 14mm)
Long frame sides L (3)	Pine	$23\frac{3}{8}$ x 2 x $\frac{3}{4}$in (594 x 51 x 18mm)
Short frame sides M (4)	Pine	$10\frac{1}{4}$ x 2 x $\frac{3}{4}$in (260 x 51 x 18mm)
Lower frame front N (1)	Pine	$23\frac{3}{8}$ x 3 x $\frac{3}{4}$in (594 x 76 x 18mm)
Drawer side support Q (2)	Pine	$12\frac{1}{4}$ x $1\frac{1}{4}$ x 1in (311 x 32 x 25mm)
Corner braces R (4)	Pine	4 x 4 x $\frac{3}{4}$in (102 x 102 x 18mm)
Castors (4), two that lock		

SLATTED SHELVES (FOR TWO SHELVES)

Long sides (4)	Pine	$24\frac{1}{8}$ x 2 x $\frac{3}{4}$in (612 x 51 x 18mm)
Short sides (4)	Pine	$12\frac{1}{4}$ x 2 x $\frac{3}{4}$in (311 x 51 x 18mm)
Slats (12)	Pine	$24\frac{7}{8}$ x $1\frac{1}{2}$ x $\frac{3}{8}$in (632 x 38 x 9mm)

DRAWER

Front (1)	Pine	$21\frac{1}{4}$ x $4\frac{15}{16}$ x $\frac{3}{4}$in (540 x 125 x 18mm)
Sides (2)	Plywood	$14\frac{1}{2}$ x $3\frac{5}{8}$ x $\frac{1}{2}$in (368 x 92 x 12mm)
Back (1)	Plywood	$21\frac{1}{4}$ x $3\frac{5}{8}$ x $\frac{1}{2}$in (540 x 92 x 12mm)
Base (1)	Plywood	$20\frac{1}{4}$ x $13\frac{1}{2}$ x $\frac{1}{4}$in (514 x 343 x 6mm)
Short base supports (2)	Pine	$12\frac{1}{2}$ x $\frac{1}{2}$ x $\frac{1}{2}$in (318 x 12 x 12mm)
Long base supports (2)	Pine	$20\frac{1}{4}$ x $\frac{1}{2}$ x $\frac{1}{2}$in (514 x 12 x 12mm)
ALSO REQUIRED:		
Pine knob (1)		

EXTENDING SHELF

Extending shelf (1)	Plywood	$22\frac{3}{4}$ x $12\frac{1}{8}$ x $\frac{1}{2}$in (578 x 308 x 12mm)
Handle (1)	Pine	$12\frac{1}{8}$ x $1\frac{1}{4}$ x $\frac{3}{4}$in (308 x 32 x 18mm)

PAPER-TOWEL ROLL POLE

Post (1)	Pine	$4\frac{1}{2}$ x $2\frac{1}{2}$in (114 x 64mm) diameter
Post dowel (1)	Hardwood	$1\frac{1}{2}$ x $\frac{1}{2}$in (38 x 12mm) diameter
Pole (1)	Pine	$10\frac{1}{2}$ x $\frac{7}{8}$in (267 x 22mm) diameter
ALSO REQUIRED:		
Pine ball (1)		$1\frac{1}{2}$in (38mm) diameter

CONSTRUCTION

TOP

1 Plane the sides of a length of 4 x 2in (102 x 50mm) pine, square and cut it up into 63 pieces. Cut seven of these in half. Arrange four blocks and one half-block in a row, end to end, ensuring that the face of the row is free of knots, and glue and clamp them securely together (see Fig 9.1).

FIG 9.1
One row of blocks, glued and clamped.

FIG 9.2
Smoothing the blocks with a block plane.

Glue up 14 of these rows. When dry, place the rows of blocks edge to edge and glue them together to form the top, selecting the knot-free faces to form the top surface. Arrange the blocks so that they look like brickwork, with the half-blocks at alternate ends.

2 When the glue is dry, plane the top surface smooth using a block plane, and plane the sides flat (see Fig 9.2). While planing, use a straight edge to check that the top surface is flat. Finish the top surface with rough and then smooth pads on a random orbital sander.

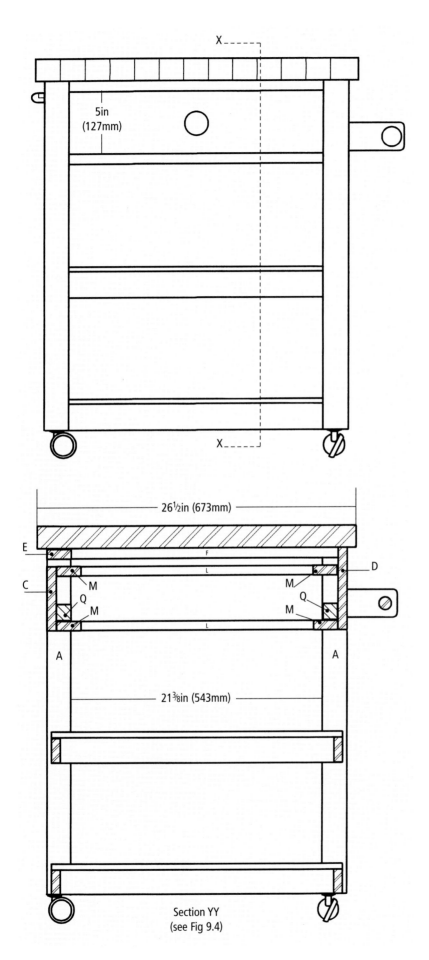

5in
(127mm)

X

X

26½in (673mm)

E

F

C

M

L

M

D

Q

M

M

Q

A

A

21⅜in (543mm)

Section YY
(see Fig 9.4)

FIG 9.3
Front view and section with dimensions.

CARCASS

To simplify the construction nearly all the carcass pieces are joined using dowels (see Figs 9.5 and 9.6; see also page 19).

1 Start by cutting the four legs (**A**) to the correct length, from planed 2 x 2in (50 x 50mm) pine. Cut out the deep back rail (**B**), the deep side rail (**D**) and the shallow side rail (**C**) and, using a jig, make dowelled joints to fit these to the legs. Cut out the long (front) and short (side) top rails (**G** and **E**) and form dowelled joints on the ends of these also. Where these two rails fit into the leg, the dowels are shorter on the inside of the rails – if they were the normal length, they would meet in the middle of the leg.

2 Assemble and glue the two sides (**C** and **E**) with the legs. When these are dry, join the two sides with the long rails (**B** and **G**) to make a square carcass. Check the diagonals to ensure that the assembly is square. In order to keep the legs the correct distance apart at the lower ends while clamping, cut pieces of scrap wood to length and place between them temporarily.

3 Now make the two sub-frames that fit below and immediately above the drawer. For both, cut the parts to size and make the dowelled joints, but do not cut the notches that fit around the legs in parts **L** and **N** at this stage. Glue, assemble and clamp the frame pieces together. Ensure that they are square by measuring the diagonals. Form part **F** and cut the notch in the corner, before gluing and screwing into place against part **B**. To size the corner notch accurately, use the leg as a template by holding **F** against it and marking the size of the notch. Part **F** serves as the top runner of the extension slider, as

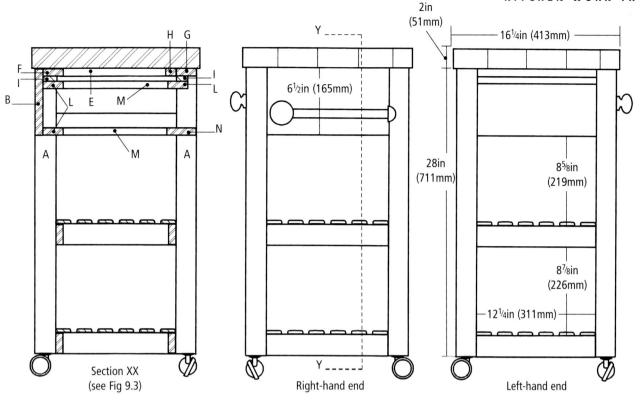

FIG 9.4
Side views and section with dimensions.

does piece **H**, which should now be cut and screwed into place.

4 Cut out parts **I**, which are two narrow strips of wood that act as spacing pieces to ensure that the gap for the slider to fit into is correct and to constrain the sides of the slider when it is in use.

Turn the carcass upside down and glue and pin parts **I** into place on the undersides of parts **F** and **G**. Hold the two sub-frames made earlier in place and mark the corner notches into which the legs are fitted. Cut out these notches and drill holes in the rails for the screws.

FIG 9.6
Using a pencil sharpener to put a point on the dowels.

5 With the carcass still inverted, glue the frame that fits immediately above the drawer and fit it into place against parts **I** with screws and glue. Fix the final sub-frame that goes under the drawer into place next. This is positioned so that it lines up with the lower edge of parts **D** and **C**, which will leave an opening 5in (127mm) deep for the front of the drawer.

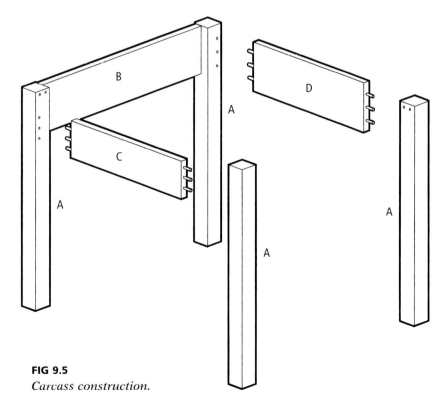

FIG 9.5
Carcass construction.

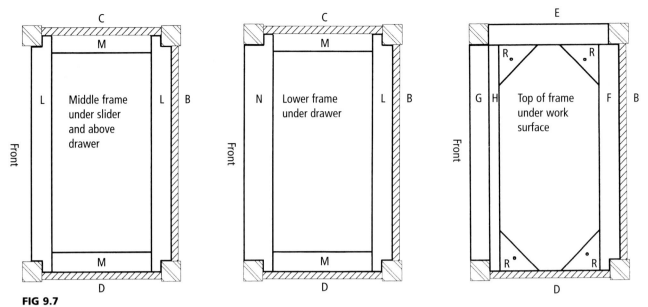

FIG 9.7
Sub-frames for drawer housing.

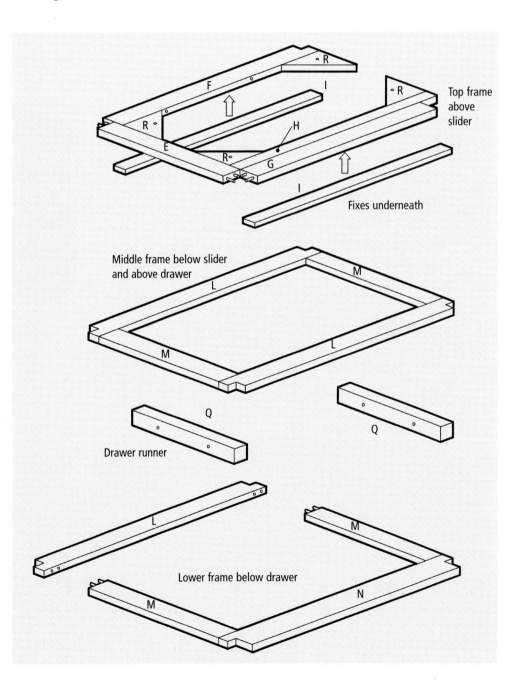

FIG 9.8
*Sub-frames
construction.*

6 Because the area that the drawer fits into is wider than the drawer, you will now need to cut two side rubbing strips (**Q**) and screw them on to the insides of pieces **C** and **D**. These will stop the drawer moving from side to side and hold it straight.

7 To brace the top of the carcass and provide a means of fixing the block top, make four corner braces (**R**) and screw them into place (see Fig 9.9). Make holes in these for the screws that will eventually be used to hold the top.

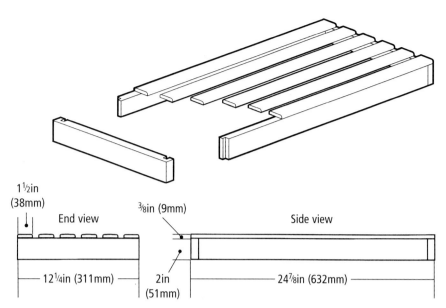

1½in (38mm) End view ⅜in (9mm) Side view

12¼in (311mm)   2in (51mm)   24⅞in (632mm)

FIG 9.10
Slatted shelf construction, plus end and side views with dimensions.

FIG 9.9
Fitting the corner braces.

SLATTED SHELVES

The construction of the two shelves built into the lower half of the trolley is exactly the same for both.

1 The joints on the corners of the frame that support the slats are bare-faced housings (see page 16), although dowels would be equally suitable. Glue and clamp the frames, ensuring that they are square. To make the slats, use planed stock such as cladding and cut into pieces 1½in (38mm) wide. Using a jack plane and glasspaper, round off the top edges and cut the pieces to length so that they are slightly longer than the frame.

2 Glue and pin the slats on to the frame and punch the heads of the pins below the surface of the wood. To cover these, fill the punch holes with a mixture of glue and wood dust and, when the filler is dry, glasspaper the surface smooth.

3 Where the ends of the slats project slightly beyond the ends of the frame, plane them flush to the frame ends with a block plane. When both shelves have been made, fit them into the carcass with a screw at each corner (see Fig 9.11).

FIG 9.11
Fitting one of the slatted shelves.

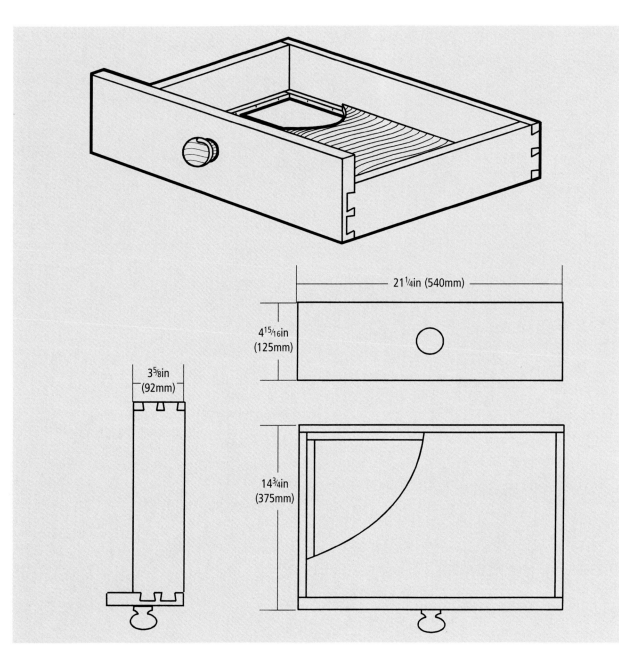

FIG 9.12
Drawer construction and plans with dimensions.

DRAWER

The drawer is flush fronted, with lapped dovetails on the front corners and through dovetails on the rear. The base is made from plywood fixed on to square-section pine strips which are glued and pinned around the inside edges of the base of the sides.

1 Cut out the drawer front and plane all the edges square. It should fit into the hole in the front of the carcass with a ¹⁄₃₂in (1mm) clearance all round.

2 Mark and cut out the back and sides, and glasspaper the edges. Following the procedure on page 18, make through dovetails on the back corners and lapped dovetails on the front corners.

3 Mark and cut out the base, making sure that it is exactly square. Cut out the base-supporting strips and glue and pin them on to the four sides on the inside bottom edge.

4 Glue and assemble the four corners and, with the base placed temporarily inside, clamp the sides. (The base will hold the sides square as the glue dries.) When the glue on the corners is dry, glue and pin the base supports around the inside of the base of the sides, and pin the base to them. Clean up the joints at the corners with a plane, and screw a wooden knob to the drawer front.

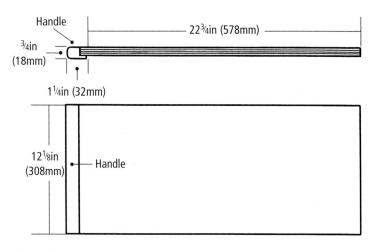

FIG 9.13
Plans of extended shelf with dimensions.

EXTENDING SHELF

The extending shelf can be deployed whenever extra surface space is required. It is made from a piece of plywood that runs the complete length of the carcass in the slot provided. It has been made this long so that it can be extended for up to 15in (381mm) from the trolley without any danger of its falling out.

1 A softwood handle is fixed on one end of the plywood. Make this by forming a rebate in a suitable piece of pine which has been cut to size and then rounded off on the front edges. Fix the handle to the shelf with glue.

PAPER-TOWEL ROLL POLE

A roll pole is fixed to the side of the trolley so that paper towels are immediately to hand when

required. The dimensions are correct for a standard-sized paper towel, but the roll pole can also be used for a tea towel if required. I made my roll pole from various pieces of dowelling and round-sectioned softwood; for example, the pole itself is a piece of pine originally intended as a broom handle. If a lathe is available, the pieces could be custom-made from the dimensions shown.

1 The 2½in (64mm) diameter pine for the post is the most difficult to obtain. I cut a length from a pole, from the centre of a roll of floor covering. When you have found or manufactured a suitable post, drill a ⅞in (21mm) hole in the side to take the pole, and a ½in (12mm) hole in the base to house the dowel. Glue the hardwood dowel into the post to fix it to the side of the trolley.

2 The knob on the end of the pole is small enough to pass through the cardboard tubing in the centre of a paper roll but slightly larger in diameter than the pole, so that the paper towel roll will not slide off the pole easily once it is on it. To make the knob, find a wooden ball of the correct size, saw it in half, and drill a hole in the flat side of one of the hemispheres for the pole to fit into. Glue the pole into the post, and the knob on to the pole.

3 Using a ½in (12mm) bit, drill a hole in the appropriate part of the side of the trolley and glue the post into place. Make sure that the pole is exactly horizontal.

ASSEMBLY AND FINISHING

1 Fix the top to the carcass with four long screws. As the screws are fixed into the end grain of the top, which is not as secure as fixing them across the grain, the extra length will compensate for any weakness. (The top was not fixed in place earlier because it is easier to get the extending shelf and the drawer to fit correctly if the top of the carcass is open.)

2 Fix the four castors (two of which lock into position) to the base of the legs with screws.

3 Apply three coats of cleat matt polyurethane varnish to the entire carcass. Because the top will be used for vegetable preparation, varnish or polish do not make a suitable finish. Instead, treat the top with a couple of applications of vegetable oil. When it has been used for vegetable preparation, wipe down with a wet cloth and occasionally retreat with oil.

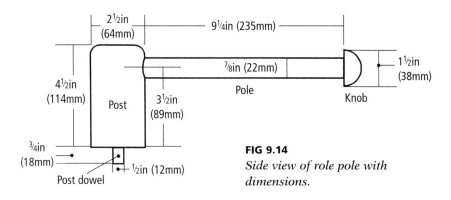

FIG 9.14
Side view of role pole with dimensions.

10 Bed headboard

DEGREE OF DIFFICULTY: EASY/MEDIUM
TIME TO MAKE: 30 HOURS

This bed headboard made in pine will complement the bedroom furniture featured in the other chapters. It is intended for fitting to a bed that is pushed up against a wall, so that the headboard will be supported if leant against.

Most beds have bolts built into them at the time of manufacture, which are for fitting a headboard. This one is designed to fix to a bed with four screws low down on the back of the bed. Because these bolts are not standard and their position might vary on a different bed, I have not given the dimensions of the slots they fit into. However, for a different arrangement it would be easy to cut a slot in another position on the headboard. Some beds do not have a facility for fitting a headboard, in which case it could be fixed with wood screws through the plywood and into the pieces of wood from which the bed is made.

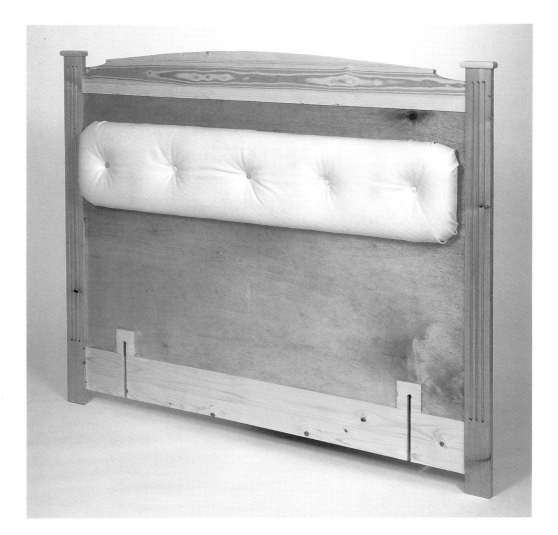

CUTTING LIST
HEADBOARD

Upright posts (2)	Pine	44¾ x 3 x 1in (1,136 x 76 x 25mm)
Top rail (1)	Pre-jointed pine board	56 x 6 x ¾in (1,422 x 152 x 18mm)
Lower rail (1)	Pre-jointed pine board	56 x 6 x ¾in (1,422 x 152 x 18mm)
Post caps (2)	Pine	4 x 1¼ x ¾in (102 x 32 x 18mm)
Headrest back board (1)	Plywood	54 x 10 x ½in (1,372 x 254 x 12mm)
Spacers (2)	Plywood	3 x 3 x ¼in (76 x 76 x 6mm)
Back board (1)	Plywood	56½ x 33 x ½in (1,435 x 838 x 12mm)
Batten supports (2)	Pine	24 x 4 x ½in (610 x 102 x 12mm)
Padded headrest covering (1)	Fabric	60 x 15in (1,524 x 381mm)
Thick padding (1)	Plastic foam	54 x 10 x 2in (1,372 x 254 x 51mm)
Thin padding (1)	Plastic foam	16 x 15 x ½in (1,524 x 381 x 12mm)
ALSO REQUIRED:		
Upholstery buttons (5)		½in (13mm)
Cord		
Dowelling (for joints)		

CONSTRUCTION

HEADBOARD FRAME

1 Cut the wood for the two upright posts to size and plane all faces square. Using a router with a ⅜in (10mm) core-box cutter, form the three ornamental flutes on the face of each post (see Fig 10.3) and then clean up with glasspaper wrapped around a piece of ⅜in (9mm) dowel (see Fig 10.4).

2 Cut the top and lower rails to length and mark the long, smooth curve on the top of the top rail. To draw this use a piece of flexible plywood about the same length as the rails. Hold it near the top of the rail, on its edge, and then bend it into the

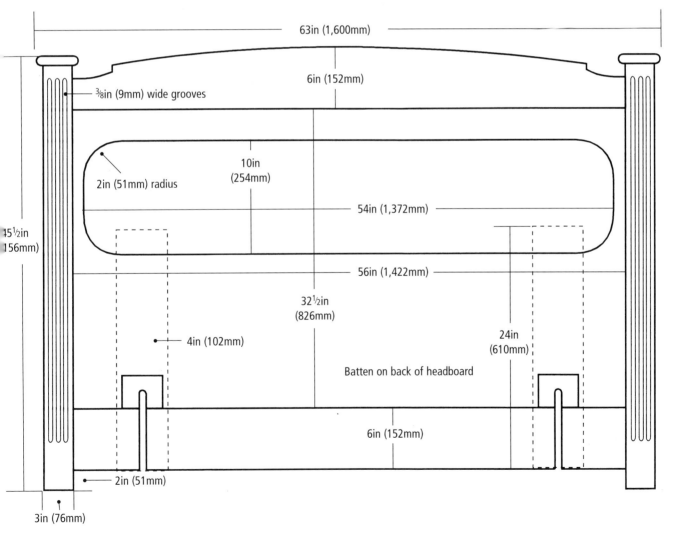

FIG 10.1
Plan of headboard with dimensions.

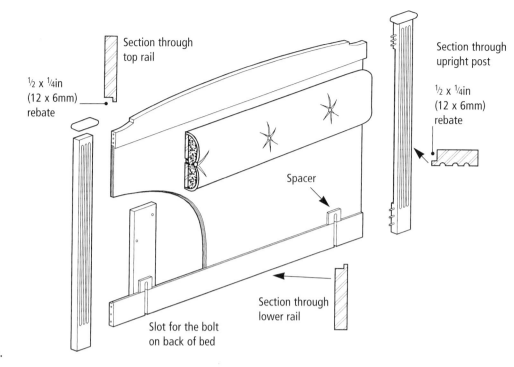

Section through top rail

½ x ¼in (12 x 6mm) rebate

Section through upright post

½ x ¼in (12 x 6mm) rebate

Spacer

Section through lower rail

Slot for the bolt on back of bed

FIG 10.2
Headboard construction.

FIG 10.3
Cutting the flutes with a router.

FIG 10.4
Smoothing the grooves with glasspaper.

Each square = 1in (25mm)

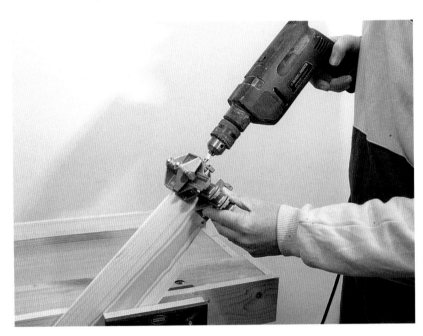

FIG 10.5
Headboard template.

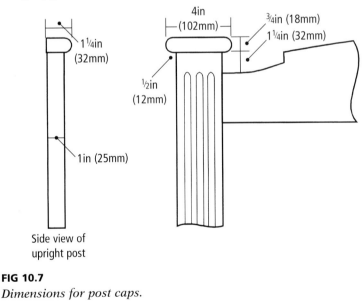

FIG 10.6
Using a jig to make a dowelled joint.

1¼in (32mm)

1in (25mm)

Side view of
upright post

4in (102mm)

¾in (18mm)

1¼in (32mm)

½in (12mm)

FIG 10.7
Dimensions for post caps.

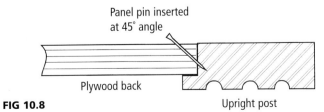

Panel pin inserted
at 45° angle

Plywood back

Upright post

FIG 10.8
Method for inserting pins.

required curve. Use a pencil to trace along its edge and mark the curve. This is a two-person job, one holding the plywood while the other draws around it. Draw the end shapes on the wood by squaring up from Fig 10.5.

3 When all the curves have been drawn, cut around them with a coping saw, or a band saw if available (which saves a lot of hard work), and smooth the shape with a rasp, file and glasspaper. Make the ends of both rails square by marking carefully with a try square before sawing.

4 Using a router with a ½in (12mm) flat cutter, cut rebates from one end to the other in the back edges of both rails, and cut stopped rebates in the inside edge of the upright posts, to house the plywood back.

5 Join the rails to the upright posts with dowelled joints (see page 19), using a dowel jig to drill the holes (see Fig 10.6). Test the joints for accuracy and then glue hardwood dowels into the upright posts.

6 Cut the wood for the two post caps to size and round off the fronts and sides with a plane. Fix the caps to the tops of the uprights with glue and pins. So that the heads of the pins do not show, punch them below the surface, fill the holes with pine-coloured filler and glasspaper smooth when dry.

7 Apply glue to the ends of the rails, then join them to the posts and clamp together.

HEADBOARD BACK

1 To make the back the correct size to fit into the frame, cut the plywood slightly oversize, place it on the floor and lay the frame over the top of it. Draw around the inside edge on to the plywood with a pencil and then cut out with a panel saw.

2 To fit the back into the frame, spread glue around the rebate, lay in the plywood back and secure it with 1in (25mm) panel pins. Because the base of the rebate is not thick enough to hold the pins, you will need to angle them at 45° so that they fix into the sides of the rebate (see Fig 10.3).

STRENGTHENING THE HEADBOARD

When a headboard is being used, it is frequently leant against when the occupant is reading in bed or drinking a beverage. It is important that the headboard is strong enough to be used in this way.

1 To strengthen the headboard, fix two battens to the back with screws and glue. The lower end of these battens also strengthens the sides of the slots in which the bolts, fitted to the bed, are held (see Fig 10.2).

2 The position of the slots depends on the arrangement of these bolts on the bed. Carefully measure their location before fixing the battens into place, and mark the position for the slots with a try square and pencil.

3 To fit the headboard to the bed, the bolts are loosened and the headboard is pushed downwards on to them. When the bolts are tightened the headboard is pulled into close contact with the back of the bed. Because there is a step between the lower rail and the plywood

back, tightening the bolts may distort the back board. To avoid this, cut two small spacing pieces and glue them to the plywood back (see Fig 10.2).

4 To cut the slot, drill a ⅜in (9mm) hole at the ends where the slots terminate. Using a panel saw, cut the sides of the slots and remove the waste wood (see Fig 10.9).

FIG 10.9
Cutting the slots with a panel saw.

PADDED HEADREST

1 Cut the headrest back board to size, and mark the radius of all four corners using a compass set at 2in (51mm). Cut these with a coping saw and smooth the edges with glasspaper.

2 Cut the thick plastic foam to the same size and shape as the board and stick the two together with impact adhesive. (Ensure

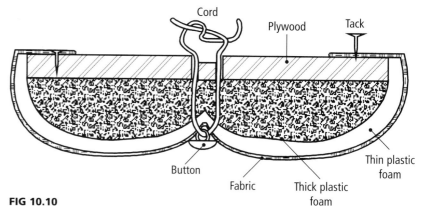

FIG 10.10
Section through padded headrest.

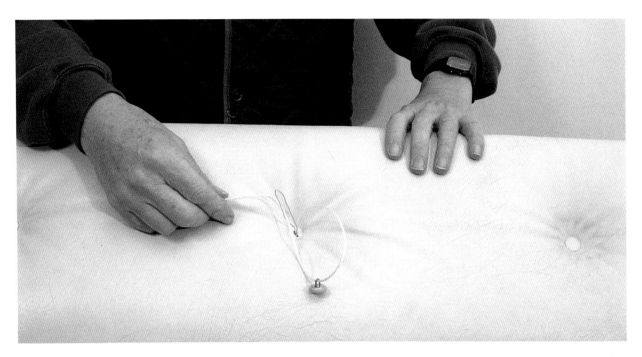

FIG 10.11
Threading an upholstery button through the headrest.

that the foam is fire retardant – it is safer and also mandatory in some circumstances.)

This type of foam is available from specialist dealers and is easily cut with a sharp carving knife, using a piece of wood as a straight edge. Should you be unable to purchase a long enough piece, simply coat the two edges to be joined with impact adhesive and allow it to dry before pushing them together.

3 Place the second piece of thin fire-retardant plastic foam on the floor and position the foam-covered board on top of it, with the foam side downward. Coat the edges of the thin foam that show underneath the padded board, and the edges of the padded board, with glue. When the glue has dried, pull the thin foam around the padded board to form a smooth, rounded shape. Trim off any overhanging foam with a sharp knife.

4 My padded headboard is covered with a plastic vinyl fabric, although other fabric, perhaps to match the curtains, would also be suitable. Lay the fabric on the floor and pull it around the board in the same way as when covering the board with thin foam. Secure the fabric with upholstery tacks fixed into the back of the plywood board.

5 Mark the positions for the buttons on the back of the plywood board. At each mark drill two ¼in (6mm) holes through the board, about ½in (12mm) apart. Remove some of the wood between the holes with a bevel-edged chisel, so that the knot of the cord which holds the buttons will settle below the surface. This ensures that the padded board sits flush into the back board when screwed into place.

6 I used upholstery buttons covered in the same fabric as the headrest. These can be obtained

from and covered by most upholsterers. They have a metal ring in the back through which a length of cord is passed. To attach the buttons to the board, push a length of wire right through one hole, the foam and the covering fabric in turn. Bend over the end of the wire to form a loop, thread the cord through the loop and pull the wire back through the cushion to the back of the board. Thread a button on to the cord and pull the second end through. Pull the cord tight and knot it: this has the effect of pulling the button into the cushion to create the 'dimpled' effect. Repeat for each button.

ASSEMBLY AND FINISHING

1 Apply several coats of clear matt polyurethane varnish to the headboard and then wax polish it.

2 Fit the headrest to the headboard with screws through the back of the back board.

11 Bedside cupboard

DEGREE OF DIFFICULTY: MEDIUM
TIME TO MAKE: 45 HOURS

This bedside cupboard is the first of a pair, one for either side of the bed. There is a generic similarity between the various pieces of the bedroom suite due to some common design features, but they are not intended to match – I am aiming for a family likeness but with different characteristics. The style is a traditional design partly based on motifs from the nineteenth century.

The size of the cupboard is dictated by the location. It needs to be a comfortable height for bedside use, with the drawer accessible when leaning from the bed.

CONSTRUCTION AND ASSEMBLY

The method used to make the carcass is board and batten construction, which is one of the simpler ways to make a cabinet. The sides of the cupboard are the 'boards' and the side pieces of the three supporting square assemblies are the 'battens'. Where wide boards are required, pre-jointed boards are more convenient than jointing them yourself.

CUTTING LIST		
CARCASS		
Sides (2)	Pre-jointed pine board	19⁷⁄₈ x 14 x ³⁄₄in (505 x 356 x 18mm)
Top (1)	Pre-jointed pine board	14³⁄₄ x 17¹⁄₂ x ³⁄₄in (375 x 445 x 18mm)
Side decorative strips (2)	Pine	14³⁄₄ x ³⁄₄ x ³⁄₄in (375 x 18 x 18mm)
Front decorative strip (1)	Pine	17¹⁄₂ x ³⁄₄ x ³⁄₄in (445 x 18 x 18mm)
Side battens base and top (4)	Pine	13⁵⁄₁₆ x 1 x ³⁄₄in (339 x 25 x 18mm)
Side battens mid-section (2)	Pine	13¹³⁄₁₆ x 1 x ³⁄₄in (351 x 25 x 18mm)
Front and back rails base and top (4)	Pine	14¹⁄₂ x 1¹⁄₂ x ³⁄₄in (368 x 38 x 18mm)
Front rail mid-section (1)	Pine	14¹⁄₂ x 2 x ³⁄₄in (368 x 50 x 18mm)
Back rail mid-section (1)	Pine	14¹⁄₂ x 1¹⁄₂ x ³⁄₄in (368 x 38 x 18mm)
Facing strips (2)	Pine	14¹⁄₂ x ¹⁄₂ x ³⁄₄in (368 x 12 x 18mm)
Back (1)	Plywood	19⁷⁄₈ x 14⁷⁄₈ x ³⁄₁₆in (505 x 378 x 4mm)
Left-hand door (1)	Pre-jointed pine board	11¹³⁄₁₆ x 7¹⁄₂ x ³⁄₄in (300 x 190 x 18mm)
Right-hand door (1)	Pre-jointed pine board	11¹³⁄₁₆ x 7¹⁄₄ x ³⁄₄in (300 x 184 x 18mm)
Cupboard floor made up from planks (1)	Pine cladding	13¹⁄₄ x 11⁵⁄₁₆ x ³⁄₈in (337 x 287 x 9mm)
ALSO REQUIRED:		
Brass butt hinges (2)		2in (50mm)
Ball catch (1)		
Door catch (1)		
Pine knobs (2)		*continued over*

FIG 11.1
Front view and side section with dimensions.

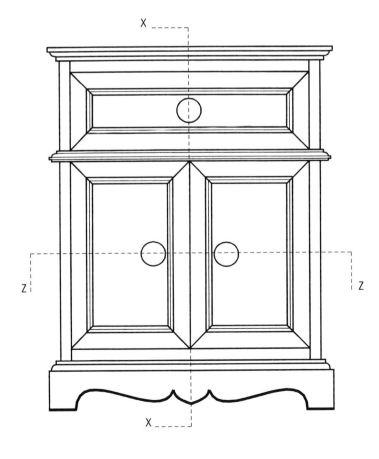

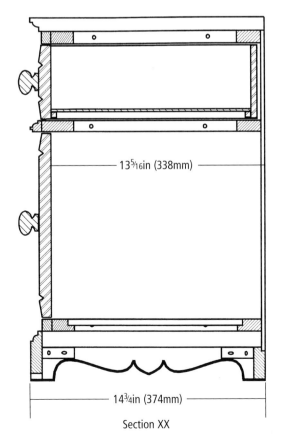

13⁵⁄₁₆in (338mm)

14³⁄₄in (374mm)

Section XX

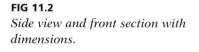

CUTTING LIST CONTINUED		
PLINTH		
Front (1)	Pine	$17\frac{1}{2}$ x 3 x $\frac{3}{4}$in (444 x 76 x 18mm)
Back (1)	Pine	16 x 2 x $\frac{3}{4}$in (405 x 51 x 18mm)
Side (2)	Pine	$14\frac{3}{4}$ x 3 x $\frac{3}{4}$in (374 x 76 x 18mm)
Braces (4)	Pine	$2\frac{1}{2}$ x $2\frac{1}{2}$ x $\frac{3}{4}$in (64 x 64 x 18mm)
DRAWER		
Front (1)	Pre-jointed pine board	$14\frac{3}{8}$ x $4\frac{9}{16}$ x $\frac{3}{4}$in (365 x 116 x 18mm)
Side (2)	Pine	$13\frac{3}{4}$ x $4\frac{9}{16}$ x $\frac{3}{8}$in (349 x 116 x 9mm)
Back (1)	Pine	$14\frac{3}{8}$ x $4\frac{9}{16}$ x $\frac{3}{8}$in (365 x 116 x 9mm)
Base (1)	Plywood	$13\frac{5}{8}$ x $12\frac{7}{8}$ x $\frac{3}{16}$in (346 x 327 x 4mm)
Base support strips front and back (2)	Pine	$13\frac{5}{8}$ x $\frac{3}{8}$ x $\frac{3}{8}$in (346 x 9 x 9mm)
Base support strips sides (2)	Pine	$12\frac{1}{8}$ x $\frac{3}{8}$ x $\frac{3}{8}$in (308 x 9 x 9mm)
ALSO REQUIRED:		
Pine knob (1)		

FIG 11.2

Side view and front section with dimensions.

FRAMES

1 Prepare the pieces for these assemblies to thickness and width. To make the corner bridle joints (see page 25), mark the ends of each piece using a marking gauge, try square and marking knife, and then cut them with a tenon saw. Test the joints for fit and modify them if necessary. (Note that the battens for the top and base assemblies do not reach the front of the cabinet but stop short; a facing strip is glued on to the front to hide the bridle joints. The battens for the middle assembly *do* run to the front, because the bridle joints will be hidden by the decorative strip which will be fixed over them.) Before the joints are glued, drill and countersink the screw holes in the side battens; these are used when the battens are fixed to the sides.

2 Glue and assemble the components for all three frames. Ensure that each one is square and exactly the correct size. If required, the size can be modified slightly after gluing with a jack plane.

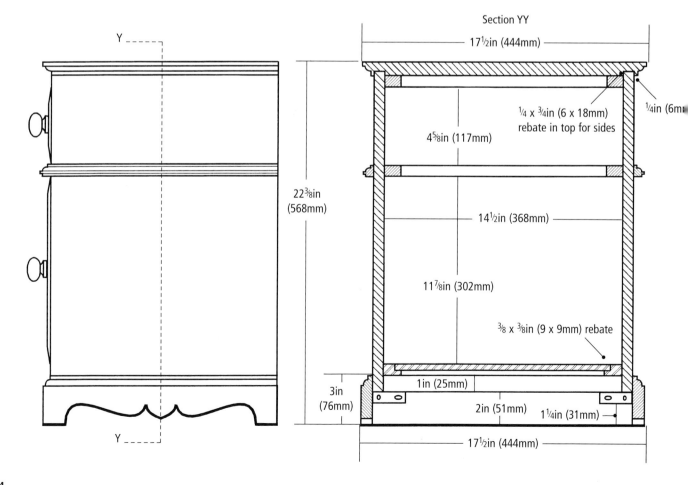

FIG 11.3
Section through middle of cupboard with dimensions.

$^3/16$ x $^3/16$in (4 x 4mm) rebate

$^3/16$in (4mm) plywood

4$^1/2$in (110mm)

11$^5/16$in (287mm)

Section ZZ
(see Fig 11.1)

SIDES

1 Cut out the two sides and mark the positions of the frame assemblies on the inside of both.

2 Using a rebating plane, make rebates on the back inside edge of both sides, where the back panel will be fitted.

3 Hold the frames on to the sides in the marked positions and fix with screws.

FIG 11.4
Frame construction.

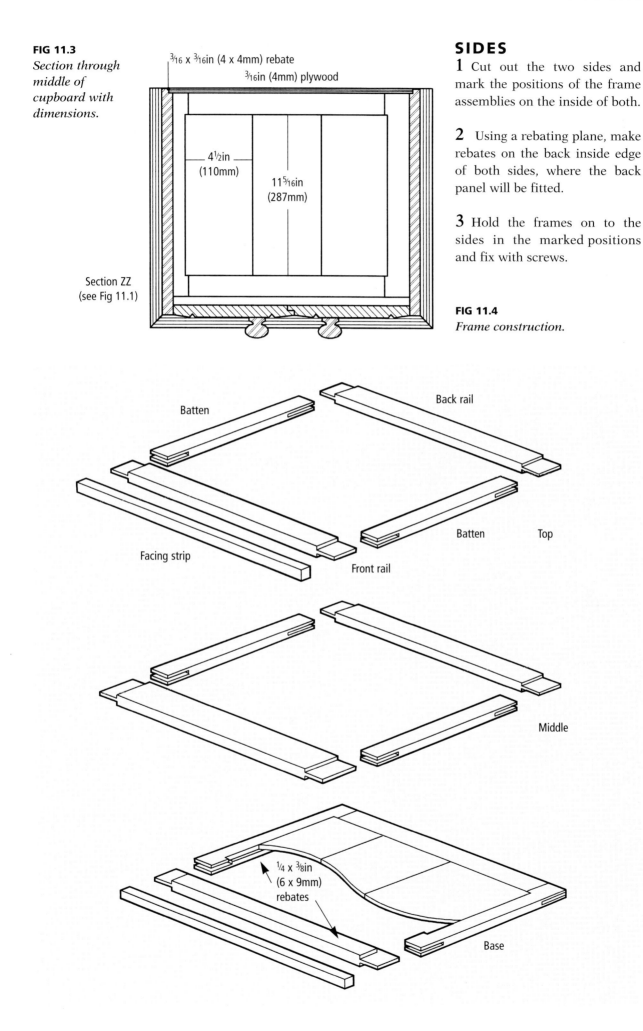

Batten

Back rail

Facing strip

Batten

Top

Front rail

Middle

$^1/4$ x $^3/8$in (6 x 9mm) rebates

Base

75

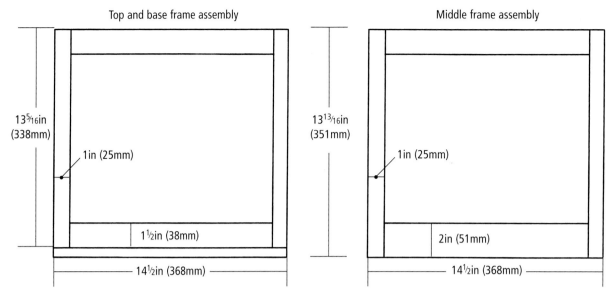

Top and base frame assembly

Middle frame assembly

13⁵⁄₁₆in (338mm)

1in (25mm)

1¹⁄₂in (38mm)

14¹⁄₂in (368mm)

13¹³⁄₁₆in (351mm)

1in (25mm)

2in (51mm)

14¹⁄₂in (368mm)

FIG 11.5
Frame plans with dimensions.

PLINTH

1 Prepare enough stock for the front and two sides of the plinth and use a router to cut the decorative shape on the top edge. Cut it into three pieces and make the mitre joints on the two front corners. Cut the back to size and make a rebate in the top edge to house the back panel. The joint between the back and the two sides is a simple butt joint.

2 The ornamental shaping on the front and the sides is an opportunity for a little creativity, but you can use the exact shaping shown if you would like to. To do this, you will need to make a card pattern by squaring up from Fig 11.6. Cut these shapes out and use them as templates to draw the shapes on to the plinth components, then cut them out with a coping saw (see Fig 11.7).

Note that the size of the shape shown in Fig 11.6 refers to the size of the back of the pieces and does not make allowances for the

FIG 11.6
Plinth construction and template for front and sides.

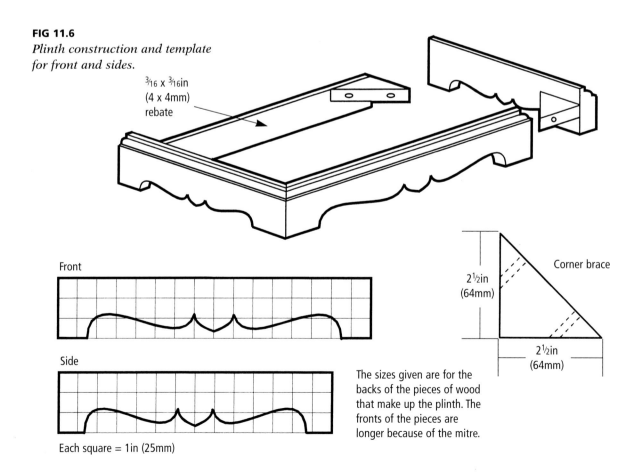

³⁄₁₆ x ³⁄₁₆in (4 x 4mm) rebate

Front

Side

Each square = 1in (25mm)

2¹⁄₂in (64mm)

Corner brace

2¹⁄₂in (64mm)

The sizes given are for the backs of the pieces of wood that make up the plinth. The fronts of the pieces are longer because of the mitre.

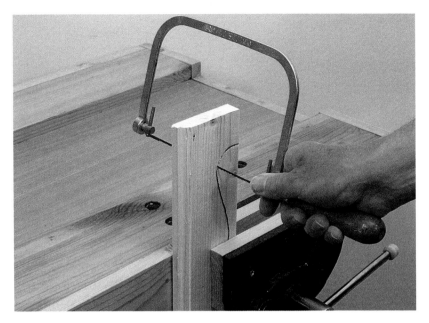

FIG 11.7
Cutting the ornamental shaping for the plinth with a coping saw.

FIG 11.8
Fitting the carcass into the plinth.

extra wood required for the mitre joints.

Smooth the shapes using the method of your choice – I used a drum sander for the long, smooth curves and a small half-round file for the tight corners.

3 The simple butt joints on the back corners are strengthened with triangular braces, which also form a platform for the carcass to stand on. Cut out the braces and screw and glue them into place, then test that the carcass fits into the plinth (see Fig 11.8).

4 Prepare the facing strips and glue them on to the fronts of the frames. Cut rebates in the back and the front rail of the lower frame to house the floor of the cupboard (see Fig 11.4). Cut the tongue and groove cladding boards for the floor of the cupboard to size and glue them into place.

TOP

1 Cut the top to size, with the grain direction running from side to side, and once again use the router to make the moulded edge.

2 On the underside, mark and cut the two grooves that house the top edges of the sides of the carcass. The depth of these grooves is such that the top cross rails of the carcass will rest against the underside of the top when the sides are fully installed in the grooves.

3 Cut slots in the top battens of the carcass so that the top can be fixed with screws fitted with washers. The slots will allow for any movement of the top caused by changes in temperature or humidity. The top is not glued.

FIG 11.9
*Front view of cupboard doors
with dimensions.*

¼ x ¼in (6 x 6mm)
rebates to form overlap

1in (25mm)

³⁄₈in (9mm) wide
shaped groove

11¹³⁄₁₆in
(298mm)

7½in (190mm)

7¼in (184mm)

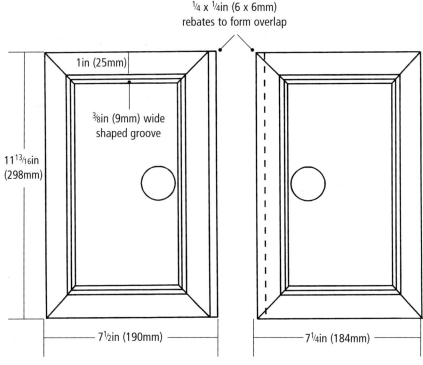

BACK

Make the back by measuring the recess it occupies, cutting it out and then fixing it to the cupboard with panel pins.

DECORATIVE MOULDING

1 To make decorative moulding that runs around the carcass, cut a length of pine sufficient to make two sides and a front, including enough spare length to allow for the mitres on the two front corners, and then cut the moulding along the complete length. I used a combination of a rebate made with a rebating plane and a cut made by a moulding bit in a router to achieve the shape shown (see pages 72 and 73). As with the other decorative features of the cupboard, there is some scope here for individual creativity. Cut the length of moulding into three and make the mitres using a mitre block. Glue the decorative strip into place.

FIG 11.10
Fixing the hinges on to the doors.

DOORS

1 Cut the two door pieces to size and form a rebate on one edge of both to make an overlap. On the front of each door, make the decorative groove using a router fitted with a 'V' groove cutter. Clean up the corners of the groove with a bevel-edged chisel. (These grooves can be cleaned up with glasspaper on a shaped block if they do not cut cleanly.) Form a slope on the face of the

doors between the decorative groove and the edge by chamfering with a plane.

2 Ensure that the doors fit into the carcass with approximately ¹⁄₃₂in (1mm) clearance all round, and then mark out the positions of the hinges one hinge length from the top and bottom of the doors. Cut the recesses in the carcass to house the hinges (see Fig 11.10) and fit them carefully

FIG 11.11
Making the hinge housings in the carcass.

FIG 11.12
Drawer plans and section with dimensions.

so that the doors hang correctly. If they do not, the hinge recesses may have to be adjusted. As the heads of the brass screws used are easily damaged, fit the hinges initially with steel screws (see Fig 11.11) and replace these with brass ones when fitting is complete.

3 The door knobs shown (see page 72 and right) were turned on my lathe, but you can buy them ready made. They were turned two at a time and then separated while still on the lathe. Fix the knobs to the doors with screws.

2 Fix a small catch in place to hold the doors closed. I used a small brass ball catch which can be adjusted to ensure that the doors close satisfactorily.

DRAWER

1 Cut out the drawer front with the grain direction running from top to bottom, so that it matches the grain direction for the sides and cupboard doors. The drawer front should fit into the hole in the front of the cabinet with a $\frac{1}{32}$in (1mm) clearance all round. On the face of the front, cut the same decorative groove and chamfer as on the cupboard doors.

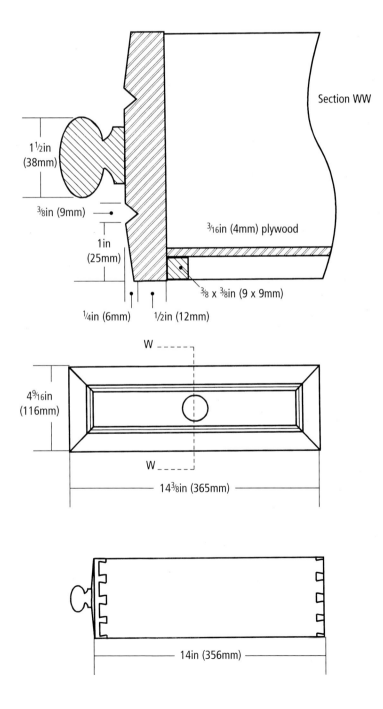

Section WW

$\frac{3}{16}$in (4mm) plywood

$1\frac{1}{2}$in (38mm)

$\frac{3}{8}$in (9mm)

1in (25mm)

$\frac{3}{8}$ x $\frac{3}{8}$in (9 x 9mm)

$\frac{1}{4}$in (6mm) $\frac{1}{2}$in (12mm)

W

$4\frac{9}{16}$in (116mm)

W

$14\frac{3}{8}$in (365mm)

14in (356mm)

FIG 11.13
Drawer construction.

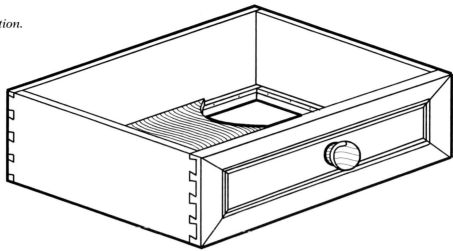

2 Mark and cut out the drawer back and sides. Make through dovetails on the two back corners of the drawer and lapped dovetails on the two front corners (see page 19). Test the joints for fit.

3 Cut out the base as square as possible. Hold the base in place in the drawer temporarily, to enable the sides to be glued up as squarely as possible.

4 Cut out the support strips and glue and pin them around the bottom edge of all four sides of the inside of the drawer to support the base. Glue the base into place.

5 Clean up all the joints with a jack plane (see Fig 11.14). Screw a knob to the centre of the drawer front.

FINISHING

As for all the pieces for the bedroom, the wood is left its natural colour and varnished with three coats of clear matt polyurethane varnish. This type of varnish is ideal here because the top of the cupboard will be required to withstand the occasional mug of hot cocoa.

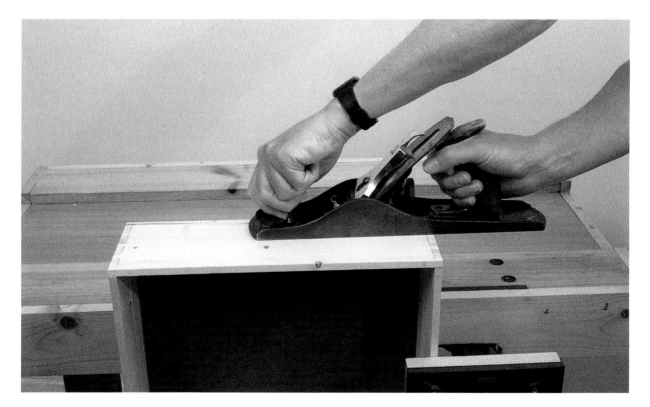

FIG 11.14
Cleaning the dovetails with a jack plane.

12 Chest of drawers

DEGREE OF DIFFICULTY: MEDIUM
TIME TO MAKE: 50 HOURS

This chest of drawers is part of a suite of bedroom furniture made in a traditional style. Each part of the suite bears a 'family' resemblance to the other pieces, but is not intended to be an exact match. The plan is to create a set of furniture which looks as though it was collected over a number of years; the individual pieces harmonize with and complement each other, but if necessary each one can stand alone.

Each side of the chest is a wide board made up from tongue and groove planks, and these are connected by three frames to make up the carcass. This sits upon a shaped plinth and houses four drawers. The top is another wide board made up from smaller planks. The drawers are side hung with inserted false fronts.

CUTTING LIST

CARCASS

Front and back rails for all frames (6)	Pine	29½ x 2 x ¾in (749 x 50 x 18mm)
Side rails for top and bottom frames (4)	Pine	16⅞ x 1½ x ¾in (428 x 38 x 18mm)
Side rails for middle frame (2)	Pine	16⅛ x 1½ x ¾in (409 x 38 x 18mm)
Side panels, made from tongue and groove planks 114 x 4½in (3m x 114mm) (2)	Pine	27⁵⁄₁₆ x 17⅛ x ¾in (694 x 435 x 18mm)
Drawer runners (8)	Hardwood	15½ x ⅞ x ⅞in (394 x 22 x 22mm)
Top, made from planks 140 x 5¾in (3,556 x 146mm) (1)	Pine	33 x 18 x ¾in (838 x 457 x 18mm)
Back (1)	Plywood	29⅞ x 27¼ x ³⁄₁₆in (759 x 692 x 4mm)
ALSO REQUIRED:		
Dowelling (for joints)		

PLINTH

Sides (2)	Pine	17¾ x 4 x ¾in (451 x 102 x 18mm)
Back (1)	Pine	30¾ x 2¾ x ¾in (781 x 70 x 18mm)
Front (1)	Pine	32¼ x 4 x ¾in (819 x 102 x 18mm)
Corner blocks (4)	Pine	2½ x 2½ x 1in (64 x 64 x 25mm)

LARGE DRAWERS (FOR THREE DRAWERS)

False fronts (3)	Pre-jointed pine board	29⁷⁄₁₆ x 6¼ x ¾in (748 x 159 x 18mm)
Sides (6)	Plywood	14¾ x 5⅝ x ½in (375 x 143 x 12mm)
Backs and fronts (6)	Plywood	28⁵⁄₁₆ x 5⅝ x ½in (719 x 143 x 12mm)
Bases (3)	Plywood	27⁵⁄₁₆ x 13¾ x ³⁄₁₆in (694 x 349 x 4mm)
Long base support strips (6)	Pine	26⁵⁄₁₆ x ½ x ½in (668 x 12 x 12mm)
Short base support strips (6)	Pine	13¾ x ½ x ½in (349 x 12 x 12mm)
Central base supports (3)	Pine	14¾ x 2 x ½in (375 x 50 x 12mm)
ALSO REQUIRED:		
Pine knobs (6)		

SMALL DRAWER

False front (1)	Pre-jointed pine board	29⁷⁄₁₆ x 5¼ x ¾in (748 x 133 x 18mm)
Sides (2)	Plywood	14¾ x 4¹⁵⁄₁₆ x ½in (375 x 126 x 12mm)
Back and front (2)	Plywood	28⁵⁄₁₆ x 4¹⁵⁄₁₆ x ½in (719 x 126 x 12mm)
Base (1)	Plywood	27⁵⁄₁₆ x 13¾ x ³⁄₁₆in (694 x 349 x 4mm)
Long base support strips (2)	Pine	26⁵⁄₁₆ x ½ x ½in (668 x 12 x 12mm)
Short base support strips (2)	Pine	13¾ x ½ x ½in (349 x 12 x 12mm)
Central base support (1)	Pine	14¾ x 2 x ½in (375 x 50 x 12mm)
ALSO REQUIRED:		
Pine knobs (2)		

CONSTRUCTION

CARCASS

1 To make the two sides, cut tongue and groove planks slightly longer than finished size and glue and clamp them together to make boards that are slightly oversize (see Fig 12.4). From these compound boards, mark and cut out two rectangles to the final size. Mark the top, inside and front edges to indicate their position. On the inside face of both sides, carefully measure and mark the positions for the frames and the drawer runners.

2 On the inside back edges of the sides, use a rebate plane to cut a rebate ³⁄₁₆ x ³⁄₁₆in (5 x 5mm) to house the plywood back.

3 Because they will be subject to high levels of wear, the drawer runners are made from hardwood; I used rectangular-sectioned ramin, which is readily available from most DIY outlets. Cut the hardwood to length and shape the runners using a rebating plane (see Fig 12.5).

FIG 12.1
Front and side view with dimensions.

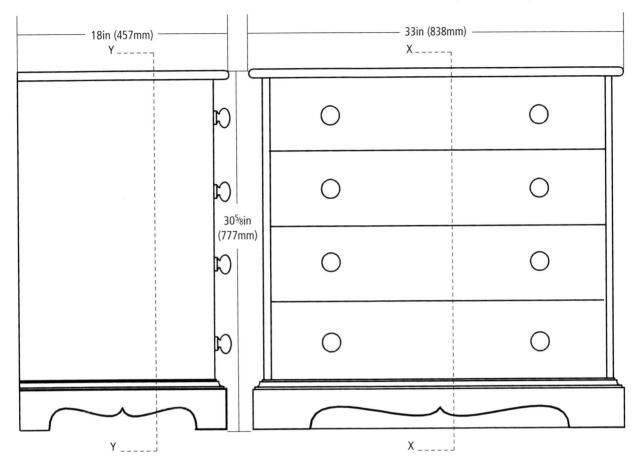

FIG 12.2
Side and front sections with dimensions.

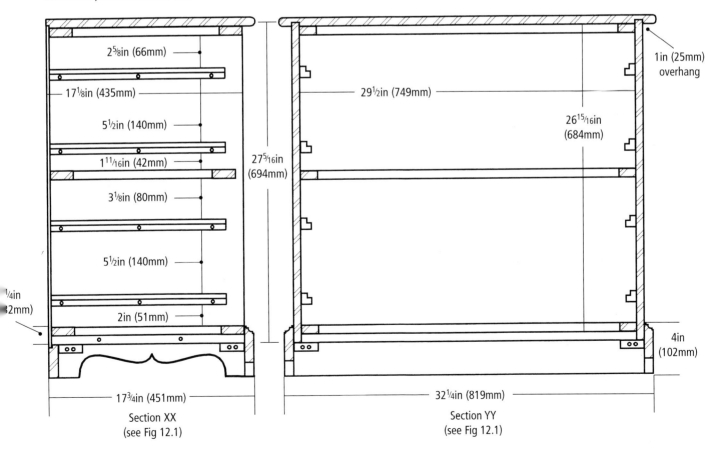

Section XX
(see Fig 12.1)

Section YY
(see Fig 12.1)

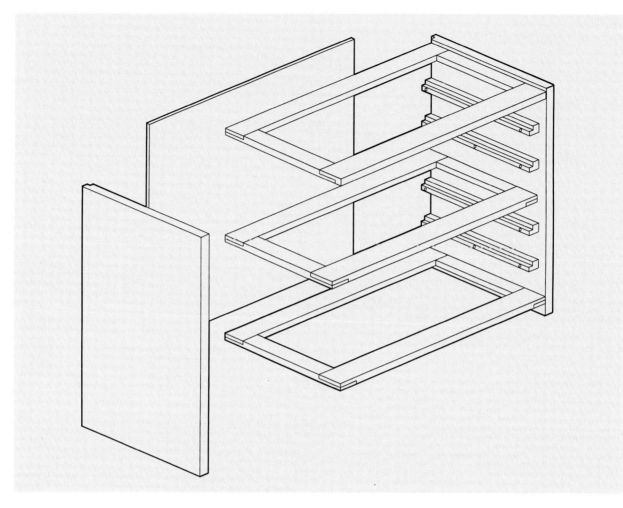

FIG 12.3
Carcass construction.

FIG 12.4
Sash cramps are used to hold the tongue and groove planks for the sides while the glue dries.

FIG 12.5
Dimensions for drawer runners.

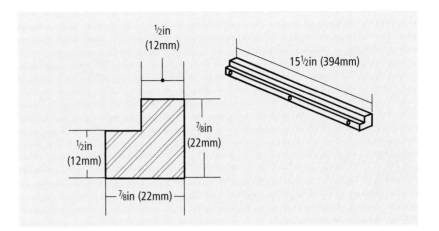

Drill and countersink the holes for the fixing screws and screw the runners to the inside faces of the sides in the marked positions. Do not glue. The screw heads should be sunk well down into the runners so that they will not interfere with the drawer movements. The runners also function as battens to hold the sides flat and help prevent warping.

4 Cut all the rails for the three frames to the required width and length and mark halving joints on the ends using a marking gauge, try square, pencil and marking knife (see page 24).

The front joints on the top frame are stopped halving joints, because the front of the frame shows in the finished chest above the drawers and the end grain of a through halving joint would look unsightly. Cut the joints with a tenon saw and glue them together, ensuring that they are set square (see Fig 12.7). A single screw will help to hold the joint.

Once dry, clean up the joints with a plane and compare the frames to make sure they are all exactly the same size. If they are not, reduce the larger ones with a plane until they are. If the joints were made carefully, any adjustments will be slight – a few passes with the plane should be enough.

Middle frame

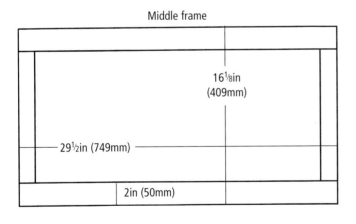

16⅛in (409mm)

29½in (749mm)

2in (50mm)

Scale 6:1

Top & bottom frame

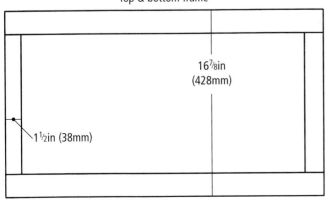

16⅞in (428mm)

1½in (38mm)

FIG 12.6
Dimensions and joints for frames.

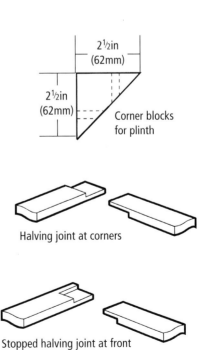

2½in (62mm)

2½in (62mm)

Corner blocks for plinth

Halving joint at corners

Stopped halving joint at front corners of top frame

FIG 12.7
A frame shortly after gluing.

FIG 12.8
The carcass ready to be fitted into the plinth.

5 The middle frame is slightly narrower than the top and bottom frames. This is because it should be set back from the front to allow for the drawer fronts. Fit the top and bottom frames into the carcass so that they extend to the front, above and below where the drawers will fit. Screw the frames into place but do not glue (see Fig 12.8).

6 Mark and cut out the back accurately. Getting it square is important, because when pinned and glued into the rebates in the back edge of the sides it ensures that the carcass will be square.

PLINTH

1 Cut a length of pine to width for the front and two sides. Along the top edge, work an ornamental moulding with a router, using the combined cuts from a straight and core-box bit. Cut the wood into three pieces for the front and two sides. Make the templates for the decorative cutouts by squaring up the shapes from Fig 12.10 on to a piece of card and then cutting out the profile. You need only produce a template for one half of each shape: draw one side on to the wood by tracing around the template, then turn it over, move it to its new position and trace out the second half. Cut out the shapes with a coping saw and smooth with a spokeshave and a half-round file (see Fig 12.11).

2 The corners of the plinth are all butt joints reinforced with blocks; at the front they are mitred and at the back they are square-ended butts. Mark and cut the mitres at both ends of the front section and at the front edge of the two side sections. The back of the plinth is a simple unadorned rectangular shape with a rebate to house the back (see Fig 12.9).

3 Cut out the four corner blocks and drill holes in them for the screws. These blocks will reinforce the butt joints on the corners and also support the base of the carcass. Fix them into place with screws and glue. Fit the carcass into the plinth and secure with screws.

TOP

1 A wide board is required for the top of the cabinet, but this time it is not made from tongue and groove board because the tongue and groove would be visible on the end grain of the top. Instead, join a number of planks using dowelled edge-to-

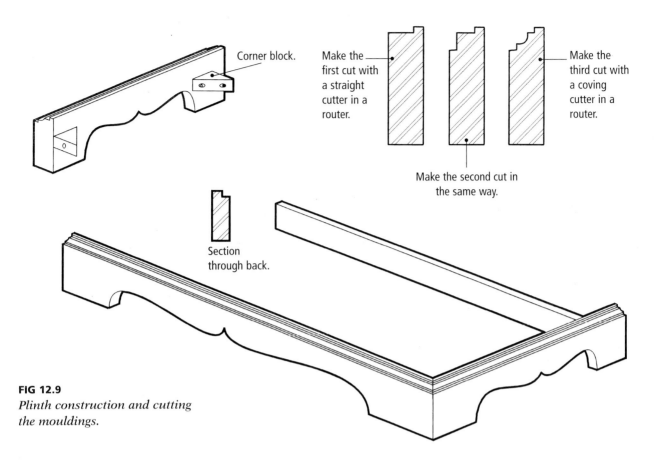

Corner block.

Make the first cut with a straight cutter in a router.

Make the third cut with a coving cutter in a router.

Make the second cut in the same way.

Section through back.

FIG 12.9
Plinth construction and cutting the mouldings.

edge joints (see page 21) to make a slightly oversize board. When assembled, cut it to the correct size and round off the edges of the front and two sides with a jack plane.

2 On the underside of the top, make two grooves with a router to house the top edges of the sides of the carcass, and make a

rebate in the underside of the back edge to accommodate the back. Fit the top into place and secure with screws that pass through holes drilled in the top frame of the carcass.

DRAWERS

The construction method for all four drawers is the same, but the top drawer has slightly less

depth. The drawers are plywood boxes with a false front made from pine. All the corner joints are through dovetails (see page 18), but any of the methods described in Chapter 4 would be acceptable. The drawers are side hung (see page 15) and because they are quite wide, have a central supporting bar, called a muntin, under the base.

FIG 12.10
Plinth template.

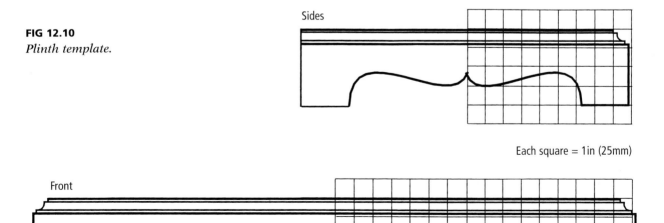

Sides

Each square = 1in (25mm)

Front

FIG 12.11
Smooth the decorative curves after they have been sawn to shape.

FIG 12.12
Plans for drawers with dimensions.

and on the front and back, mark and cut the pins. Assemble all four sides without gluing and make any necessary adjustments to the joints. Cut the large dovetails on the ends of the muntin and, with the four sides still assembled, mark the position of the large dovetail housing on the bottom edge of the front and back using the tails as a template. Cut out these housings using tenon and coping saws. Glue up the sides and muntin and, when dry, clean up with a plane.

1 For each drawer, cut a length of plywood to the correct width and lengths to make a front, two sides and a back. While the two sides are in one piece, cut the rebate for the drawer runners with a router, and then separate to make the two sides. On these sides, mark and cut the dovetails,

2 Cut the long and short strips to support the base of the drawer from square-sectioned pine. Glue and pin these strips around the inside bottom edge of the drawer. Cut out the base and glue and pin it into place on these strips. Fit all the drawers into the carcass and adjust the runners if they do not run smoothly. An

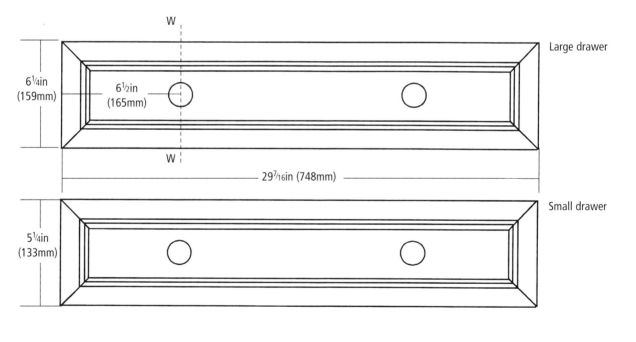

Large drawer

6¼in (159mm)

6½in (165mm)

W

W

29⁷⁄₁₆in (748mm)

Small drawer

5¼in (133mm)

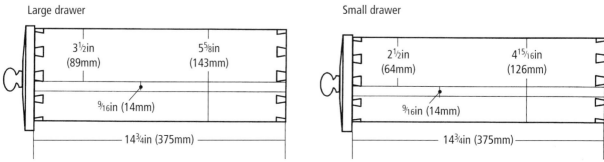

Large drawer

3½in (89mm)

5⅝in (143mm)

⁹⁄₁₆in (14mm)

14¾in (375mm)

Small drawer

2½in (64mm)

4¹⁵⁄₁₆in (126mm)

⁹⁄₁₆in (14mm)

14¾in (375mm)

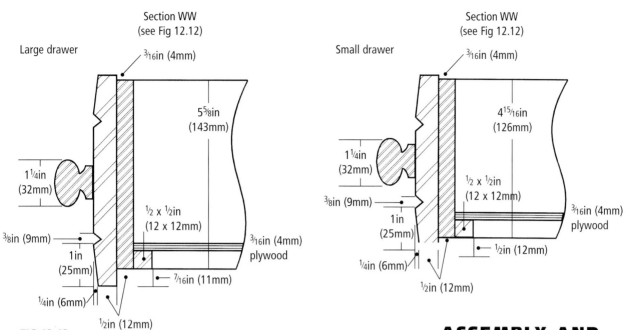

FIG 12.13
Sections through drawer fronts with dimensions.

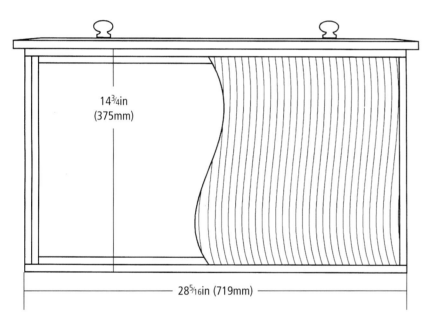

FIG 12.14
Plan view of drawer with dimensions.

application of wax will help if the drawers stick. Remove the drawers from the carcass.

3 Cut the drawer fronts to size and length and work the decorative groove using a router with a 'V'-groove cutter. Chamfer the face of the front between the decorative groove and the edge with a plane, and clean up the corners of the 'V' grooves with a sharp chisel. In the front pieces of the plywood drawers, make holes for the screws that will join them to the false fronts.

ASSEMBLY AND FINISHING

1 Fit all the drawers into the carcass and stick the false fronts on to them with some form of temporary adhesive, such as double-sided sticky tape, so that they can be moved until an exact fit is obtained. When their position is satisfactory, from the inside of the drawers mark the screw positions on the backs of the drawer fronts with a bradawl. Take the pine fronts from the drawers and apply some woodworking glue, then screw them to the plywood drawer fronts in the marked positions. Fix two knobs to each drawer front.

2 Apply three coats of clear matt polyurethane varnish to the completed chest of drawers.

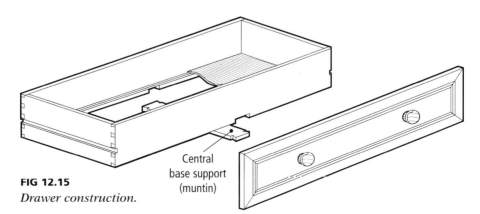
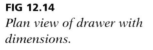

FIG 12.15
Drawer construction.

Central base support (muntin)

13 Blanket chest

DEGREE OF DIFFICULTY: MEDIUM
TIME TO MAKE: 40 HOURS

Chests were the most common pieces of furniture used in the Middle Ages. Their prime function was storage, but they also served as seats, tables and even beds. At that time only the rich could afford furniture, and because many of them travelled from one dwelling to another, chests were very practical. They would carry their belongings strapped to the backs of horses, and when they stopped for the night use them as furniture.

Many other items of furniture were developed from these chests, but in their original form they are still popular today. This blanket chest would be recognizable to a citizen of the Middle Ages, as it is a design that has stood the test of time.

CUTTING LIST

CARCASS

Base (1)	Plywood	28½ x 13⅛ x ³⁄₁₆in (724 x 333 x 4mm)
Long base supports (2)	Pine	28½ x ½ x ½in (724 x 12 x 12mm)
Short base supports (2)	Pine	12⅛ x ½ x ½in (308 x 12 x 12mm)
Long sides (2)	Pre-jointed pine board	30 x 14 x ¾in (762 x 356 x 18mm)
Short sides (2)	Pre-jointed pine board	14⅝ x 14 x ¾in (371 x 356 x 18mm)
Lid (1)	Pre-jointed pine board	31½ x 16 x ¾in (800 x 406 x 18mm)
Battens (3)	Pine	13¼ x 1⅝ x ¾in (337 x 41 x 18mm)

PLINTH

Short sides (2)	Pine	16⅛ x 3¼ x ¾in (409 x 82 x 18mm)
Long sides (2)	Pine	31½ x 3¼ x ¾in (800 x 82 x 18mm)
Corner braces (4)	Pine	2½ x 2½ x ¾in (64 x 64 x 18mm)
ALSO REQUIRED:		
Brass piano hinge (1)		28½in (724mm)
Brass ball catch (1)		
Brass lid stay (1)		

CONSTRUCTION

CARCASS

1 Cut the four sides to width and length and plane all the edges square and flat. Mark each of the sides to indicate the top edge and the outside of each piece; also mark the adjacent edges that will be joined together. Make dovetails on these edges (see Figs 13.4, 13.5, 13.6; see also page 18). From Fig 13.3 it can be seen that the tails are much wider than the pins. This is for appearances and to emphasize the hand-made look, as in most machine-made dovetails the pins and tails are the same width. Fit the joints together and make any necessary adjustments, but do not glue.

2 Now slope the top edge of the back of the chest to house the piano hinge. To help get the correct slope, set a marking gauge to the thickness of the hinge knuckle and use this to scribe a line along the outside of the top edge. Plane down the edge to the line on one side only to make the correct-sized gap for the hinge. (It is usual to recess a hinge into both the lid and the side, but that is not possible in this case because the lid overhangs the back of the chest.)

3 Glue the sides and clamp with sash cramps while the glue sets. Before this happens, take care to ensure that the carcass is square by measuring the diagonals.

Clean up the joints with a plane, and fill any gaps in the joints and blemishes on the board with a proprietary pine-coloured plastic wood. When dry, smooth the entire carcass with a random orbital sander.

FIG 13.1
Front view with dimensions.

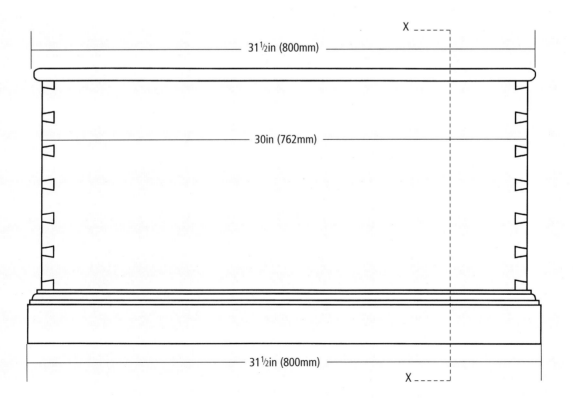

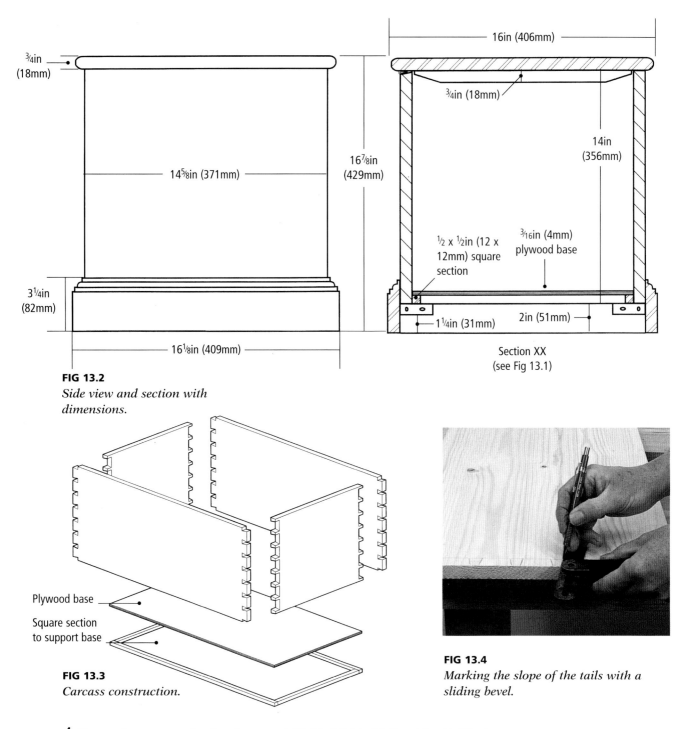

FIG 13.2
Side view and section with dimensions.

FIG 13.3
Carcass construction.

Plywood base

Square section to support base

FIG 13.4
Marking the slope of the tails with a sliding bevel.

4 To get the correct size for the base, invert the carcass on to the plywood sheet and draw around the inside edge of it with a pencil. An identification mark made on one edge of the carcass and one edge of the plywood base will make it easier to fit them together later. Cut around the pencil outline with a panel saw and smooth the edges with glasspaper.

FIG 13.5
Cleaning out the corners of the tails with a bevel-edged chisel.

FIG 13.6
Chopping out the waste between the pins with a bevel-edged chisel.

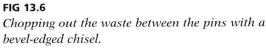

Braces screw and glue into corners

Corner braces for plinth

2½in (64mm)

2½in (64mm)

FIG 13.7
Plinth construction and corner brace dimensions.

5 Cut the long and short base supports to length to fit around the inside bottom edge of the carcass. Pin and glue them into place to support the base, then pin and glue the base on to them.

PLINTH

1 Cut the four sides of the plinth to the correct width, but slightly longer than required, to allow for the mitres to be formed in the ends. Work a moulding in the top edge using a router with a beading cutter (see Fig 13.8). Measure the inside length between the mitres on each end from the length of the carcass sides and cut the mitres with a mitre block.

FIG 13.8
Cutting the decorative moulding on the plinth.

93

2 Cut out the four triangular corner braces and drill and countersink screw holes through them (see Figs 13.7 and 13.9). Fit all the parts together, without gluing, to ensure that the plinth fits the carcass. Glue the mitres, and then glue and screw the corner braces into place.

3 Fit the carcass into the plinth and secure with a few screws that pass through the base support strips into the plinth.

FIG 13.9
Assembling the plinth.

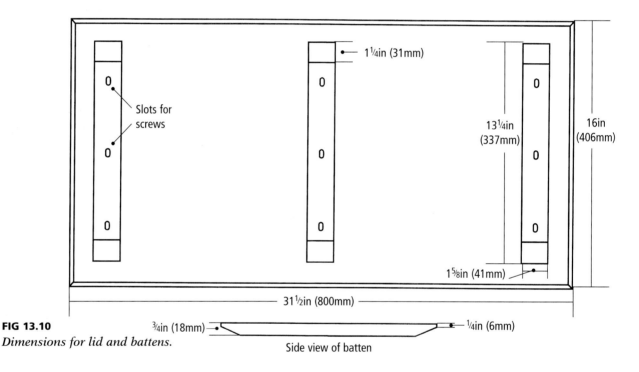

FIG 13.10
Dimensions for lid and battens.

LID

Cut the board for the lid to size, and round off the edges with a jack plane. Because the lid is simply a piece of flat board and is not supported in any way, you will need to screw three battens to the underside to prevent it warping. Make slots rather than holes in the battens for the screws, to allow the lid to shrink and expand slightly and so prevent the board from developing cracks. The battens are also used to locate the lid on to the box.

ASSEMBLY AND FINISHING

1 Cut the piano hinge to the correct length with a hacksaw and fit it to the chest and lid with brass screws. It helps if the screws are waxed before inserting them, as the heads are easily damaged if too much pressure is applied. Also fit a brass lid stay and a small brass ball catch.

2 Apply several coats of clear matt polyurethane varnish and then rub in wax polish with fine-grade wire wool.

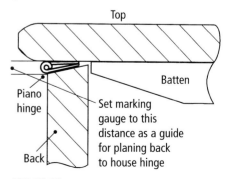

FIG 13.11
Section showing position of hinge.

14 Computer desk

DEGREE OF DIFFICULTY: MEDIUM
TIME TO MAKE: 50 HOURS

It has been estimated that within the next few years 50% of homes and nearly all small businesses will have at least one computer. This desk has been designed so that it is ideal for computer use as well as for writing letters, doing homework and household accounts, and many other aspects of home office use.

When planning a desk, the height from the floor and the height of the desk top in relationship to the height of the seat must be considered for the comfort of the user, particularly if it will be used for several hours at a time. If you have to reach upwards to the keyboard or bend your neck back to look at the monitor because the desk top is too high, you will find it tiring. If the desk is too low, you will have to stoop, which is bad for your back and could lead to injury.

In an office environment, the chairs and sometimes the desks are adjustable which alleviates most of the problems, but

for home use this is often not possible. The simple solution is to tailor the height of the desk top to the individual who will use it. The dimensions of this desk have been designed for an 'average-sized' user – between 67 and 71in (1.7 and 1.8m). For slightly taller people, the length of the uprights in the supports can be increased, while for shorter people it can be reduced.

To keep it as simple as possible, the construction makes extensive use of screws and simple joints in areas where they are not important for the visual aspects of the design. This also helps to reduce the amount of time needed to make the project.

CONSTRUCTION

TOP

The top is made from plywood, surrounded by an outer pine frame with corner bridle joints. The plywood is supported by an inner frame that is fixed inside the outer frame. Attached to the underside of this assembly is another frame, with mitred butt joints at the corner, that acts as a spacer between the top and the rectangular-shaped supports.

CUTTING LIST

TOP

Top (1)	Plywood	55 x 19 x ½in (1,397 x 483 x 12mm)
Long outer frames (2)	Pine	60 x 2½x 1½in (1,525 x 64 x 38mm)
Short outer frames (2)	Pine	24 x 2½ x 1½in (610 x 64 x 38mm)
Long inner frames (2)	Pine	55 x 1 x ¾in (1,397 x 25 x 18mm)
Short inner frames (2)	Pine	17½ x 1 x ¾in (446 x 25 x 18mm)
Inner frame cross pieces (2)	Pine	19 x 1 x ¾in (483 x 25 x 18mm)
Long spacers (2)	Pine	58½ x 1¾ x ¾in (1,485 x 44 x 18mm)
Short spacers (2)	Pine	22½ x 1¾ x ¾in (572 x 44 x 18mm)
Drawer runners (2)	Hardwood	22½ x 1¼ x 1in (572 x 31 x 25mm)

SUPPORTS ASSEMBLY

Long cross rail (1)	Pine	58½ x 2½ x 1in (1,486 x 64 x 25mm)
Cross members (2)	Pine	23½ x 2½ x 1in (598 x 64 x 25mm)
Horizontal supports (4)	Pine	24 x 2½ x 1in (610 x 64 x 25mm)
Vertical supports (4)	Pine	24¾ x 2½ x 1in (629 x 64 x 25mm)

DRAWER

False front (1)	Pine	16½ x 4¼ x ¾in (419 x 108 x 18mm)
Base (1)	Plywood	15 x 14⅝ x ³⁄₁₆in (381 x 371 x 4mm)
Sides (2)	Plywood	20 x 4 x ½in (508 x 102 x 12mm)
Front (1)	Plywood	15⅛ x 4 x ½in (384 x 102 x 12mm)
Back (1)	Plywood	15⅛ x 4 x ½in (384 x 102 x 12mm)
Long base supports (2)	Pine	15 x ½ x ½in (381 x 12 x 12mm)
Short base supports (2)	Pine	13⅝ x ½ x ½in (346 x 12 x 12mm)

1 Cut the pieces for the outer frame to length, width and thickness. Make the corner bridle joints (see page 25), test for fit, and then glue and clamp them together. Fill any holes or gaps and then clean up the joints with a plane, followed by glasspaper to achieve a good finish (see Fig 14.4).

FIG 14.1
Front view with dimensions.

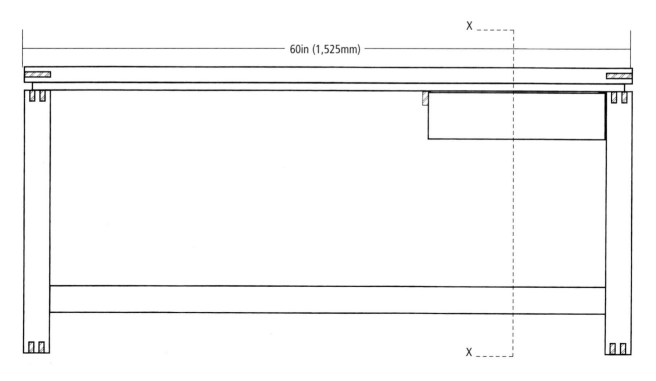

60in (1,525mm)

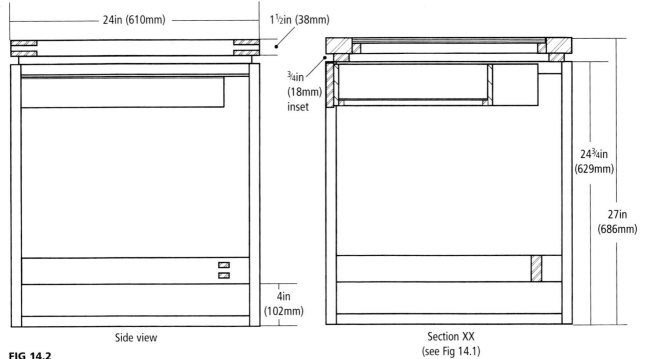

24in (610mm)

1½in (38mm)

¾in (18mm) inset

24¾in (629mm)

27in (686mm)

4in (102mm)

Side view

Section XX
(see Fig 14.1)

FIG 14.2
Side view with dimensions.

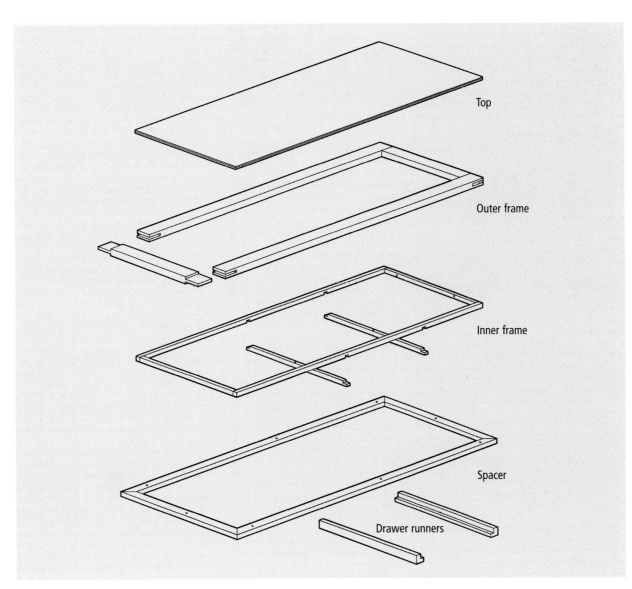

Top

Outer frame

Inner frame

Spacer

Drawer runners

FIG 14.3
Top construction.

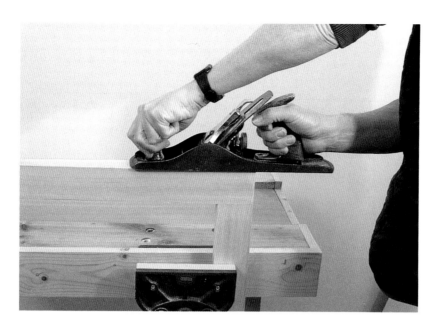

FIG 14.4
Cleaning up a corner bridle joint.

FIG 14.5
Marking the position of the inner frame with a marking gauge.

2 Place the frame over the sheet of plywood from which the top will be cut and draw around the inside edge to mark the size and shape to be cut out, so that it fits the frame. Indicate the sides of the frame that correspond to the edges of the plywood with an identifying mark and then cut out the top. Try the top in the frame for size and adjust the edges with a plane if required, to achieve a snug fit.

3 Use a marking gauge to indicate around the inside edge of the outer frame where the top of the inner frame will be positioned (see Fig 14.5). The distance from the top of the frame will be ½in (12mm), which corresponds to the thickness of the plywood top.

The inner frame consists of two long sides, two short sides and two cross pieces. The four sides are fixed to the outer frame with screws and glue, and the two cross pieces are joined to the long sides with halving joints. The corners of the frame are not jointed, as they are supported by being fixed to the inside edge of the outer frame.

Cut out these pieces, make the halving joints (see page 24) and drill the screw holes before fixing the sides of the frame up to the mark made on the inside of the outer frame. Glue the cross pieces in position and clamp them while the glue sets. Glue the top into place and insert the screws from underneath to pass through the inner frame.

4 To make the spacer frame, cut the spacers to width and length, form mitres on the corners, and fix them in place with glue and screws.

5 To complete the top, glass-paper all the exposed edges and smooth the top with a random orbital sander.

SUPPORTS

The desk top is supported by two rectangular-shaped assemblies which have box joints at the corners. These are strengthened by cross members that are fixed to the supports by the stub mortise and tenon. To give stability to the two supports, a long cross rail connects them. Twin through mortise and tenon joints connect the long cross rail to the two cross members in the supports.

1 Cut all the sides for both supports and the cross members to size and plane to the correct thickness. Make box joints at the corners (see page 17). Ensure that each corner joint is identified with a letter or number so that the correct pieces will always be fitted together, as the joint will be assembled several times while the fit is adjusted.

FIG 14.6
Support assembly.

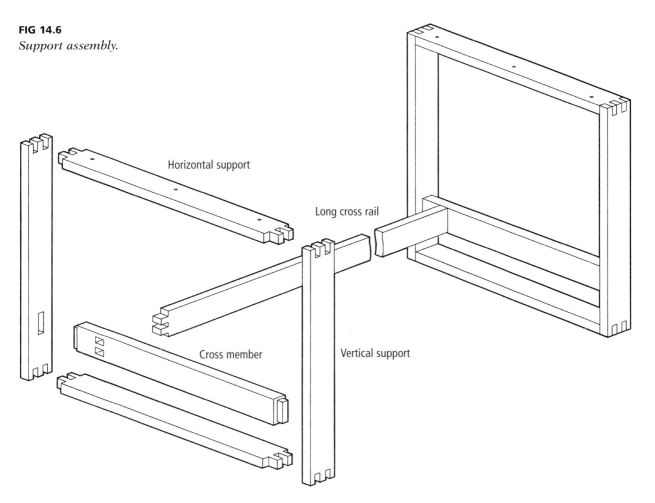

Horizontal support

Long cross rail

Cross member

Vertical support

2 Make the stub mortise and tenon joints that fix the cross members to the frame, followed by the through mortise and tenon joints that fix the long cross rail to these cross members (see page 22).

3 Glue the cross members to the vertical supports. Before the glue has time to set, glue the box joints and then clamp each frame, ensuring that they are square, until the glue has dried. Clean up all the joints and drill

the holes in the top of the horizontal supports, where they will be fixed to the underside of the top. These screw holes are offset from the centre because they fix to the centre of the spacer frame, which is set ¾in (18mm) in from the outer edge of the outer frame. Test the supports to see if they sit correctly on the spacer frame, as it is important that when they are screwed in place they are exactly at 90° to the top.

4 When this is satisfactory, glue the long cross rail to both supports and fix the supports to the underside of the top with several substantial screws and glue (see Fig 14.7). To hold the twin mortise and tenon joints at the ends of the long cross rail closed while the glue dries, I used a length of cord, tightened by twisting in a piece of wood, because I did not have a sash cramp long enough to do the job.

FIG 14.7
Screwing the supports to the top.

DRAWER

Plywood is used for the drawer construction and the sides are joined with housing joints. The drawer has a false front made of pine, and hardwood is used for the runners. The drawer sides are elongated beyond the size of the drawer so that it will be supported when it is pulled right out. This allows all the contents to be seen, with no hidden corners.

1 Cut out the two sides, back and front. Join the back to the sides with simple housing joints, then join on the front with a bare-faced housing joint (see page 16). (When you clean out the waste wood in the housings with a bevel-edged chisel, the plywood layers help to gauge the depth.)

FIG 14.8
Plans and sections of drawer and drawer runner, with dimensions.

2 Form a groove on the outside of each side for the drawer runners, using a router with a straight cutter. To tidy up any rough edges, clean out the groove with glasspaper wrapped around a block of wood (see Fig 14.10).

3 Cut the long and short strips to support the drawer base. Pin and glue these around the inside bottom edges of the sides, and then glue and pin the corner joints. Make sure that the structure is square: if not, the drawer will not slide easily. To get the correct size and shape for the base, place the assembled drawer sides on the plywood sheet and draw a pencil line around the inside edges. Cut out the base, smooth the edges with glasspaper and glue it into position.

4 Cut out the false front. Drill two holes through the front of the plywood drawer for the screws that will fix the false front to the plywood front. To position the pine front correctly, put the drawer into the desk and stick several pieces of double-sided sticky tape or other temporary adhesive to the plywood front. Hold the false front up against the plywood front and move it around until the position is correct. Once this is found, push the false front firmly against the drawer so that it is temporarily held in place. Take the drawer out of the desk and screw the false front permanently to the plywood front.

5 Cut out the two runners and use a rebating plane to form a rebate that fits into the groove in the sides of the drawer. Drill and countersink holes for the securing screws, then lubricate the runners with candle wax to ensure that the drawer slides smoothly.

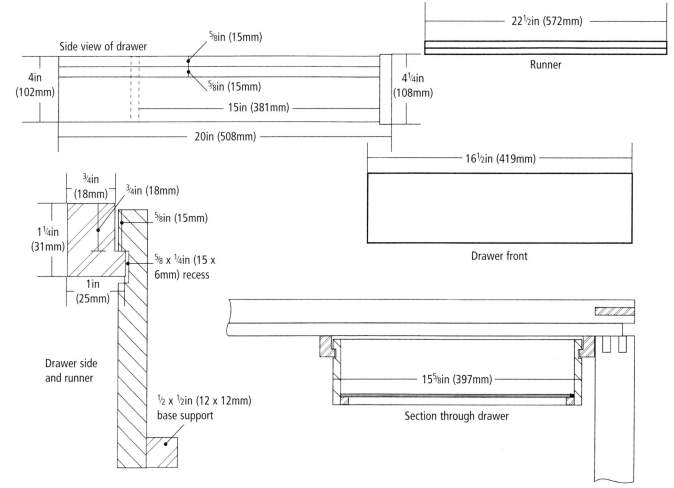

FIG 14.9
Drawer construction.

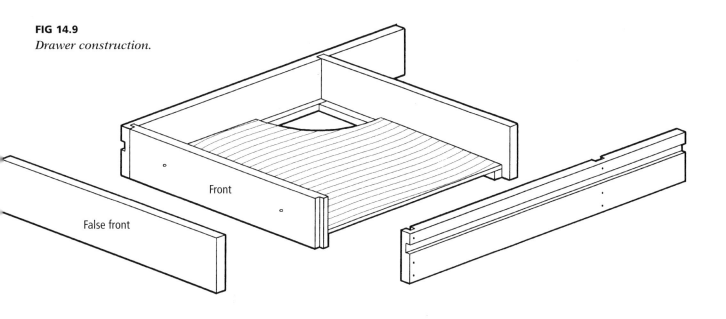

Front

False front

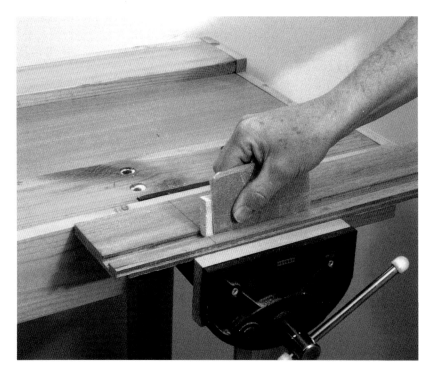

FIG 14.10
Using glasspaper to clean up the drawer runners.

ASSEMBLY AND FINISHING

1 To position the drawer runners, invert the desk and hold the runners in place in the drawer. Put the inverted drawer with runners in place on the inverted desk and mark the position where the screws will go by pushing a bradawl through the holes in the runners. Fix the runners in place with screws. There are no handles to facilitate opening and closing the drawer – it is simply pulled by hooking your fingers under the front edge.

2 Finish the entire desk with three coats of clear matt polyurethane varnish and then wax polish it to complete.

15 Chair

DEGREE OF DIFFICULTY: MEDIUM
TIME TO MAKE: 35 HOURS

This chair was made after I had completed the desk from the previous chapter, as it was apparent that a matching chair would be a worthwhile project.

Because of the difficulty of making a chair that can be adjusted to suit different people, it was tailor-made for my size (average height). To determine the various dimensions, sit at the desk on a dining-room chair and work for half an hour. If after that time no discomfort is felt, such as the seat cutting into the legs, the height is probably correct. If there is some discomfort, try sitting on a pad of some kind to raise the height, or alternatively find a slightly lower chair. When a comfortable position is found, measure the various dimensions and use these to make the chair.

For an average-sized person, the dimensions I have used should be satisfactory. I designed the chair to have arms to give the elbow support while using the computer mouse, which alleviates the ache in the shoulder that can occur if it is used for long periods. At the height specified, the chair will push under the desk when not in use.

CUTTING LIST
CHAIR

Side frame tops and bottoms (4)	Pine	17 x 2½ x 1in (432 x 64 x 25mm)
Side frame uprights (4)	Pine	24½ x 2½ x 1in (623 x 64 x 25mm)
Side frame cross rails (2)	Pine	15 x 2½ x 1in (381 x 64 x 25mm)
Front rail (1)	Pine	16 x 2½ x 1in (406 x 64 x 25mm)
Back rail (2)	Pine	16 x 2½ x 1in (406 x 64 x 25mm)
Backrest pieces (2)	Pine	17½ x 3 x 2½in (445 x 76 x 64mm)
Seat pieces (6)	Pine	16¾ x 3 x 1in (425 x 76 x 25mm)
Long seat supports (2)	Pine	17½ x 1 x ¾in (445 x 25 x 18mm)
Short seat supports (2)	Pine	13½ x 1 x ¾in (343 x 25 x 18mm)

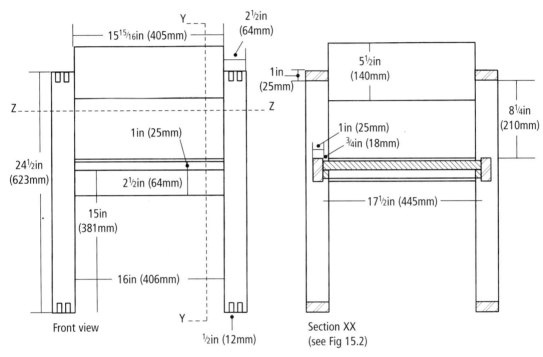

FIG 15.1
Front view and section with dimensions.

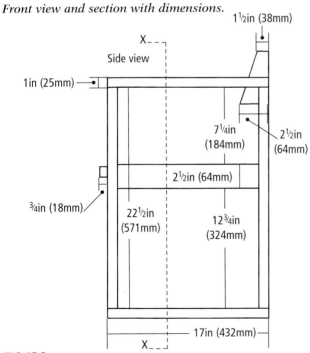

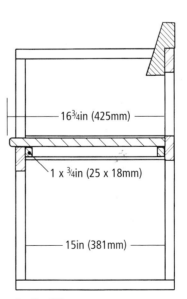

FIG 15.2
Side view and section with dimensions.

FIG 15.3
Chair construction.

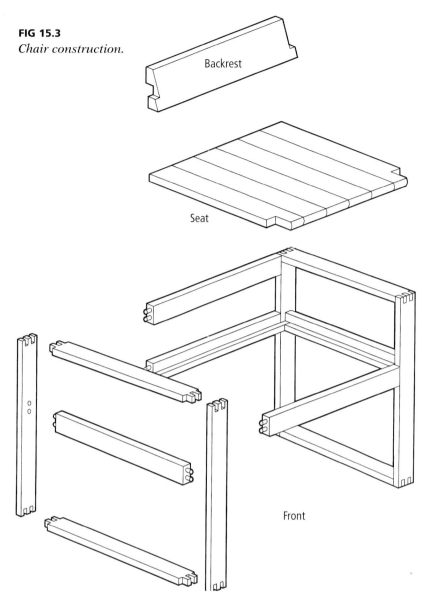

Backrest

Seat

Front

CONSTRUCTION

SIDE FRAMES

The two side frames that serve as legs, seat support and arm rests are constructed in a similar way to those that support the computer desk in Chapter 14.

1 Cut to size the eight pieces that form the two frames for the supports, which have box joints at the corners. Mark the box joints on the ends from a template made from thin plywood (see Fig 15.4) and then make the joints (see page 17). Try them for fit, and match up pairs of joints that fit well. Identify them, so that when the frames are assembled the same pairs will be joined together each time. For this I use identification letters A, A, B, B, etc. However, I never use D, as it can look like an A when viewed from the side and could lead to joining the wrong pieces together.

FIG 15.4
Using a template to mark a box joint.

2 Cut to size the two cross rails that strengthen the supports. Mark the position they will occupy inside the frame and form ⅜in (9mm) dowelled joints where the ends fit to the inside of the frames (see page 19). Assemble dry to test for fit (see Fig 15.5). Glue, assemble and clamp both frames, then clean up the joints with a jackplane, followed by glasspaper.

3 Cut out the three rails that connect the two frames: one rail goes at the front of the seat, one at the back, and one below the backrest. Using a jig, make ⅜in (9mm) dowelled joints to fix these rails to the frames. When these joints fit, glue, assemble and clamp them together.

4 Cut the long and short strips that will fit around the inside of the frame to support the seat. Drill holes for the screws that fix the seat to the supports (see Fig 15.6). Also drill and countersink further holes so that you can fix the supports into place with screws as well as glue.

FIG 15.5
Assembling one side of the chair.

FIG 15.6
Fixing the seat supports with screws.

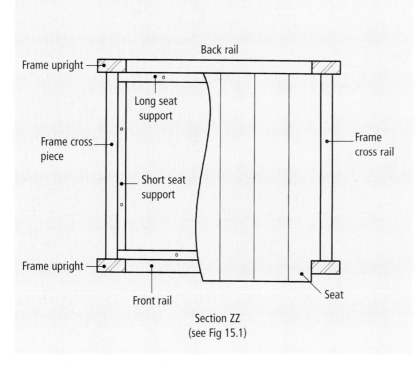

FIG 15.7
Chair seat plan section.

SEAT

1 Cut six pieces of pine each measuring 17 x 3 x 1in (431 x 77 x 25mm). Ensure that the edges are square to the faces, because the pieces are jointed with dowelled edge-to-edge joints and if the edges are not square there will be gaps between the planks.

2 Make the dowelled joints (see page 21) and then glue and clamp with sash cramps until set. Plane the top and bottom surfaces flat and finish the top surface with a random orbital sander.

3 Because I wanted the seat to fit exactly into the frame without any unsightly gaps around the edges, I made a template for the seat shape from stiff card. It is easy to get the card to fit exactly, because it is easily cut and extra pieces can be attached if too much is removed, which is far more difficult with wood. It is not important if the resulting template is a collage of small pieces, as long as it fits correctly. Draw around the template to mark the shape for the seat on to the wood. Cut out the seat and fit it to the seat supports with glue and screws. Use glasspaper held on a block to smooth the end grain on the edges.

BACKREST

To make the backrest, two pieces of 3 x 2½in (77 x 64mm) sawn pine are dowelled together so that a rebate is formed which fits over the rear rail. The lower part of the backrest has two lugs that protrude under the arm rests and butt up against the rear of the side frames. This is so that the weight of a person leaning against the backrest is spread on to the frames and not all taken on the back rail. Because of these lugs, the lower of the two pieces is longer than the top one.

1 Join the two pieces together with dowels (see page 21) and assemble them without glue. Using a sliding bevel, mark lines on the ends at 10° to vertical. Take the two pieces apart and cut along their length following the 10° line. Assemble the two pieces once again, present the back to the frame, mark the exact position of the two lugs and cut away any unwanted wood from the lower piece.

2 When the backrest fits snugly in position, take it apart and glue the parts permanently together. Plane all the surfaces flat and pay particular attention to getting the end grain smooth. Glue the backrest into place.

FINISHING

As the chair is intended to match the desk, finish it by applying three coats of clear matt polyurethane varnish.

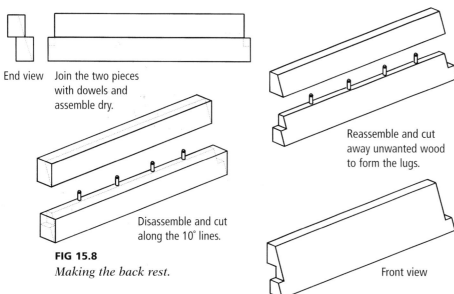

End view · Join the two pieces with dowels and assemble dry.

Disassemble and cut along the 10° lines.

Reassemble and cut away unwanted wood to form the lugs.

Front view

FIG 15.8
Making the back rest.

16 Desk drawer unit

DEGREE OF DIFFICULTY: MEDIUM
TIME TO MAKE: 30 HOURS

This desk drawer unit was made to complement the desk. It is the same width as the drawer in the desk and it will normally be positioned under the drawer. However, because it is on castors it can be pulled forwards and the top used as an extra surface on which to place papers and books.

The size of the drawers reflects the items they are intended to hold. The bottom drawer is the deepest and is just the right size for floppy disks, while the shallower drawers are intended for pens, paper, envelopes and all the usual home office bits and pieces. The depth of the unit is governed by the distance between the front of the desk and the rail at the back, as it is intended to be pushed under the desk.

CUTTING LIST

CARCASS

Sides (2)	Pre-jointed pine board	17⅜ x 15 x ¾in (441 x 381 x 18mm)
Top (1)	Pre-jointed pine board	16⅛ x 15 x ¾in (409 x 381 x 18mm)
Base (1)	Pre-jointed pine board	16⅛ x 15 x ¾in (409 x 381 x 18mm)
Drawer runners (6)	Hardwood	14 x ½ x ⁷⁄₁₆in (356 x 12 x 10mm)
Back (1)	Plywood	16⅜ x 15⅛ x ¼in (416 x 384 x 6mm)
ALSO REQUIRED:		
Castors (4), two that lock		

BOTTOM DRAWER

Sides (2)	Plywood	14⅛ x 6 x ⁷⁄₁₆in (359 x 152 x 10mm)
Front (1)	Plywood	13¾ x 6 x ⁷⁄₁₆in (349 x 152 x 10mm)
Back (1)	Plywood	13¾ x 6 x ⁷⁄₁₆in (349 x 152 x 10mm)
False front (1)	Pre-jointed pine board	16⅛ x 6⅞ x ¾in (409 x 174 x 18mm)
Base (1)	Plywood	13¾ x 13⅜ x ¼in (349 x 340 x 6mm)
Handle (1)	Pine	16⅛ x 1⅜ x ½in (409 x 34 x 12mm)

MIDDLE DRAWER

Sides (2)	Plywood	14⅛ x 5 x ⁷⁄₁₆in (359 x 127 x 10mm)
Front (1)	Plywood	13¾ x 5 x ⁷⁄₁₆in (349 x 127 x 10mm)
Back (1)	Plywood	13¾ x 5 x ⁷⁄₁₆in (349 x 127 x 10mm)
False front (1)	Pre-jointed pine board	16⅛ x 5¼ x ¾in (409 x 133 x 18mm)
Base (1)	Plywood	13¾ x 13⅜ x ¼in (349 x 340 x 6mm)
Handle (1)	Pine	16⅛ x 1⅜ x ½in (409 x 34 x 12mm)

TOP DRAWER

Sides (2)	Plywood	14⅛ x 3⅝ x ⁷⁄₁₆in (359 x 89 x 10mm)
Front (1)	Plywood	13¾ x 3⅝ x ⁷⁄₁₆in (349 x 89 x 10mm)
Back (1)	Plywood	13¾ x 3⅝ x ⁷⁄₁₆in (349 x 89 x 10mm)
False front (1)	Pine	16⅛ x 4¼ x ¾in (409 x 108 x 18mm)
Base (1)	Plywood	13¾ x 13⅜ x ¼in (349 x 340 x 6mm)
Handle (1)	Pine	16⅛ x 1⅜ x ½in (409 x 34 x 12mm)

CONSTRUCTION

CARCASS

1 Make the carcass using wide boards. I made up some boards by edge jointing tongue and groove planks, although pre-jointed boards would be equally acceptable. Make the four wide boards for the four sides slightly longer than required and then trim the ends to the correct length, ensuring that they are exactly square.

2 Box joints were chosen for the corners, although dovetails would be just as good (see page 17). The number of pins used in a box joint is optional, but it is usual to make the protruding pins equal in width to the gaps in between.

Because all the pins and gaps are equal in width, you can 'walk' a pair of dividers across the width of the wood to divide it into an equal number of parts at both ends of each side. Use a

FIG 16.1
Front and side views with dimensions.

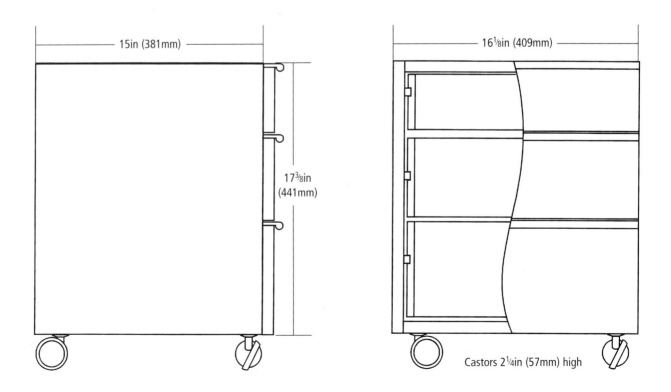

15in (381mm)

17⅜in (441mm)

16⅛in (409mm)

Castors 2¼in (57mm) high

long rule parallel to the edges to draw the lines that mark the sides of the pins. Now use a try square to draw a line at each end across the width of the board, corresponding to the thickness of the board, for the length of the pins.

Decide which boards will be jointed to each other at the corners, and indicate the pairs of joints with an identifying letter.

3 Mark the waste wood between the pins by cross hatching with a pencil (see Fig 16.3), as it is very easy to make a mistake when the pins and the gaps are the same width, and cut away the wrong parts. To make sure this does not happen, check that the waste wood between the pins on one board corresponds to the pins on the board it joins to.

Cut along the base of the waste areas, across the grain, with a marking knife. Using a tenon saw, cut the sides of the pins on the waste wood sides of the lines. Remove the waste with a coping saw: do not cut up to the line across the grain, but to within approximately ¹⁄₃₂in (1mm) of it (see Fig 16.4). To make the fine cut up to this line, use a bevel-edged chisel. Hold the chisel vertically on the line with the bevel away from you, and chop out the waste with blows from a mallet. Do this from both sides of the board, cutting through half the thickness from each side. (When doing this, make sure that the boards are lying on a clean, smooth surface, as any small wood chippings under the board will mark it and leave an indentation.) Try each pair of joints for fit and make any necessary adjustments.

4 On the back edge of the boards, cut a rebate to house the plywood back. Two of the boards have a stopped rebate and the

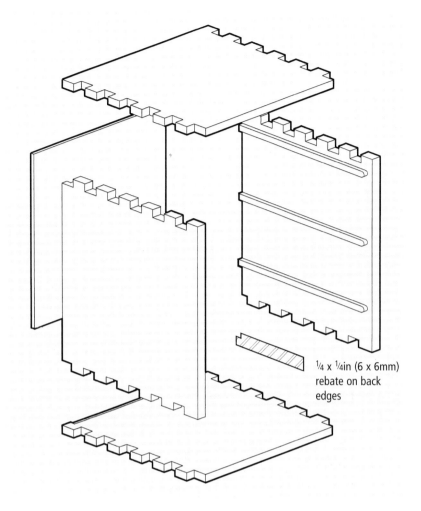

¹⁄₄ x ¹⁄₄in (6 x 6mm) rebate on back edges

FIG 16.2
Carcass construction.

FIG 16.3
Marking the areas of waste wood to be cut away.

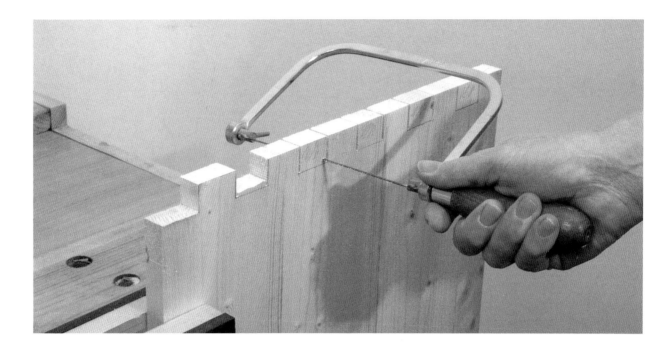

FIG 16.4
Cutting out the waste with a coping saw.

other two a through rebate. Make both of these using a router with a straight cutter. Clean up the ends of the stopped rebate with a ¼in (6mm) bevel-edged chisel.

5 To glue the carcass, spread sufficient glue on all the surfaces that butt so that it squeezes out when clamped. Because these are fairly difficult joints to glue

up and there is a limited time to do it as the glue might dry, prepare all the sash cramps in advance. You will require a minimum of four sash cramps, adjusted to approximately the correct width before gluing commences. Once the joints are clamped, wipe off any surplus glue with a damp rag, as it is much more difficult to remove it after it has dried.

When the joints have set, clean up the outside of the carcass with a smoothing plane. It is essential that the plane is

very sharp to cut the end grain on the joints and get a quality finish. Fill any gaps in the joints with pine-coloured filler and glass-paper the outside of the carcass.

6 Cut and plane the drawer runners to size. They are fixed to the inside of the carcass using glue and pins, punching the pin heads below the surface. However, do not fix the runners into place until after the drawer carcasses have been made, but do fix them before the false fronts are attached. This is because their position is found by putting the drawers into the carcass, starting with the lower one, and marking the positions of the runners from the positions of the grooves on the sides of the drawers. When the bottom runners are in place, fit the drawer and then place the middle drawer on top of it with a suitable space in between, then mark the position of the middle drawer runners. Do the same for the top drawer.

7 When all the drawer runners are in place, cut out the back of the carcass and fix it into place with glue and staples (see Fig 16.5).

FIG 16.5
Fixing the back on the carcass with a stapler.

DRAWERS

The drawers are simple plywood boxes with housing joints at the corners and 'laid on' false fronts made from pine.

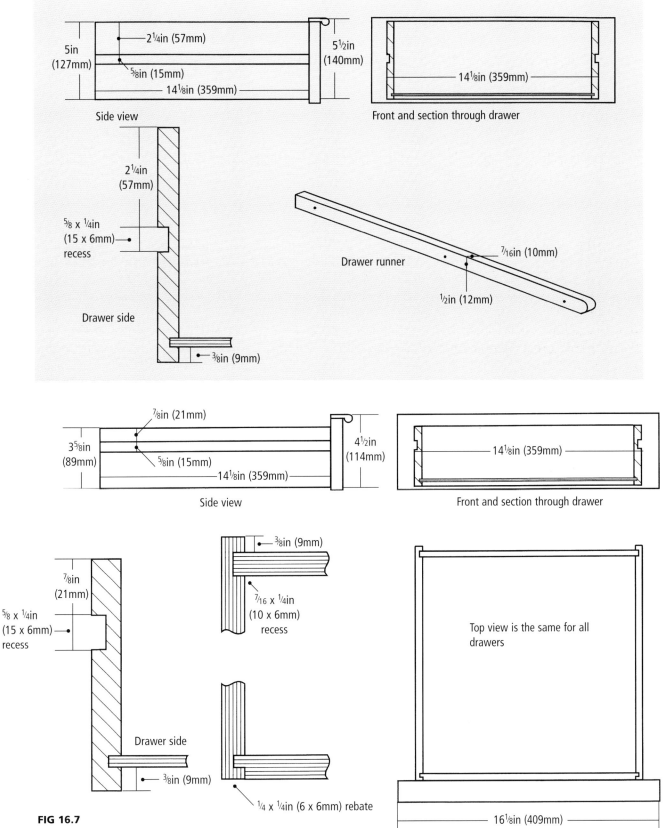

Side view

Front and section through drawer

Drawer side

Drawer runner

Side view

Front and section through drawer

Drawer side

Top view is the same for all drawers

FIG 16.7
Top drawer plans and section with dimensions.

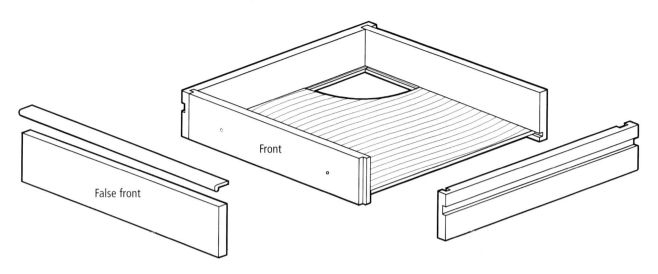

FIG 16.8
Drawer construction.

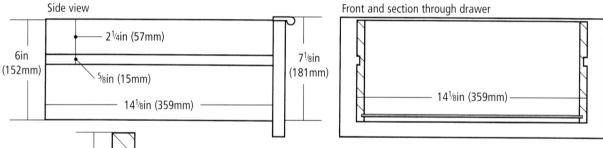

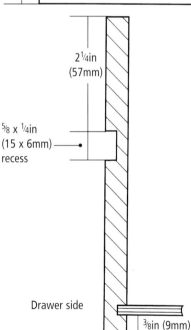

FIG 16.9
Bottom drawer plans and section with dimensions.

1 Lay out all the drawer sides on a sheet of plywood to enable them to be cut out in the most economical way. Once the best arrangement has been found, saw the sides from the sheet, and then plane all the edges smooth and square.

On the sides, but not the fronts and backs, use a router with a flat cutter to make the long grooves for the drawer runners. Adjust the fence on the router and then cut the rebates in the sides that will house the front and back of each drawer. Finally, on the inside bottom edge of the sides, front and back, cut the groove into which the plywood base will slot. Try the joints to ensure that they fit and that the drawers are square and the sides are parallel.

2 Cut out the drawer bases and try them for accuracy of fit, then glue and clamp the drawers (see Fig 16.10). Try the drawers in the carcass to ensure that they fit. Cut out the false fronts and plane the edges.

3 Cut the handle pieces to size. Form a rebate along the length of each piece, to provide the overhang on the front of the drawer which will be gripped to open the drawer. Round off the protruding part using a plane, file and glasspaper. Glue and clamp the handles to the false fronts, and then glue and screw the false fronts to the fronts of the plywood drawers. For this, you will need to drill screw holes right through the plywood fronts.

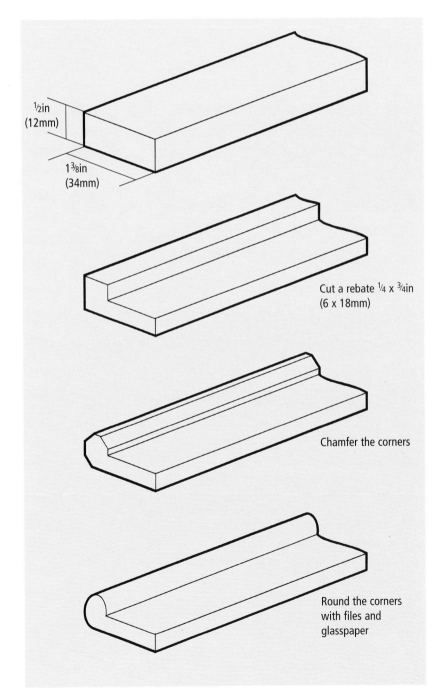

½in
(12mm)

1⅜in
(34mm)

Cut a rebate ¼ x ¾in
(6 x 18mm)

Chamfer the corners

Round the corners
with files and
glasspaper

FIG 16.10
After gluing, the drawer is clamped.

To find the position for the false fronts, put all the plywood drawers into the carcass and stick the false fronts to the plywood fronts with any temporary adhesive that will allow the front to be manoeuvred into the correct position yet is strong enough to allow the drawer to be taken from the carcass and the position of the screw holes marked. Find the position for the screws by piercing holes in the back of the false fronts using a bradawl pushed through the holes drilled in the plywood fronts. Take the false fronts off the plywood fronts, re-glue with wood-working adhesive and screw permanently into place. Glass-paper the drawer fronts, particularly the end grain.

ASSEMBLY AND FINISHING

Apply three coats of clear matt polyurethane varnish to match the desk. Fit the four castors to the base of the unit, and then lubricate the drawer runners with candle wax to complete.

FIG 16.11
Making a drawer handle.

113

17 Bookcase

DEGREE OF DIFFICULTY: MEDIUM
TIME TO MAKE: 40 HOURS

This is one of several pieces that were made to furnish a study. The size was dictated by the amount of space available after the other pieces of furniture had been accommodated, and also by the dimensions of the books it was going to hold. Because I have a number of non-fiction books that are A4 size or larger, at least one of the shelves had to be high enough for these.

It would be possible to customize the design according to individual requirements. For example, it could be made narrower or slightly wider, or an extra shelf could be added. If it was intended to hold paperbacks, the shelves could be made closer together. If a much wider version was made, the shelves would then require some extra means of support in the centre to prevent sagging.

With the exception of the back, the entire bookcase is made from ¾in (18mm) nominal thickness pine, with the various lengths and widths cut from wide pre-jointed boards. The timber was carefully selected to avoid boards with too many knots or flaws.

CUTTING LIST

PLINTH

Wide leg sides (outer stand) (4)	Pine	5½ x 2½ x ¾in (140 x 64 x 18mm)
Narrow leg sides (outer stand) (4)	Pine	5½ x 1¾ x ¾in (140 x 44 x 18mm)
Short rails (outer stand) (2)	Pine	7 x 2½ x ¾in (179 x 64 x 18mm)
Long rails (outer stand) (2)	Pine	25 x 2½ x ¾in (635 x 64 x 18mm)
Short rails (inner stand) (3)	Pine	9¾ x 2 x ¾in (258 x 51 x 18mm)
Long rails (inner stand) (2)	Pine	28½ x 2 x ¾in (724 x 51 x 18mm)
ALSO REQUIRED:		
Dowelling (for joints)		

CARCASS

Sides (2)	Pre-jointed pine board	30 x 12 x ¾in (762 x 305 x 18mm)
Top (1)	Pre-jointed pine board	30 x 12 x ¾in (762 x 305 x 18mm)
Base (1)	Pre-jointed pine board	30 x 12 x ¾in (762 x 305 x 18mm)
Shelf (1)	Pre-jointed pine board	29¼ x 11 x ¾in (743 x 279 x 18mm)
Back made from tongue and groove planks	Pine	approx. 276 x 3¾ x ⅜in (7,000 x 95 x 9mm)

FIG 17.1
Side view and front section with dimensions.

CONSTRUCTION

PLINTH

The plinth is made up of two stands: an outer one, of which the legs are an integral part, and an inner one that adds strength, holds the carcass clear of the outer stand and adds the ½in (12mm) gap which gives visual interest to the design.

1 Cut the eight pieces of timber that are required to make the four legs to length and width, square them up with a plane and join the corners of each pair of pieces that make one leg, using dowels (see page 25). Glue and then clamp them together, and while waiting for them to dry, cut the two long and two short rails to size.

2 Dowel and glue the rails to the legs, using sash cramps to hold them in position. Before the glue is set, check the diagonals of the stand to ensure that it is square.

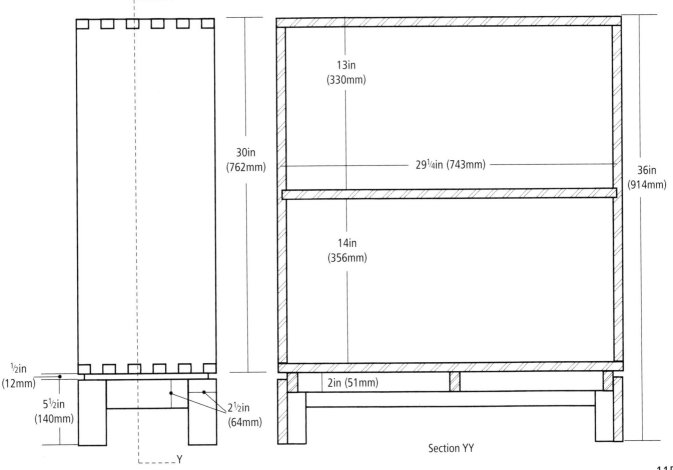

Section YY

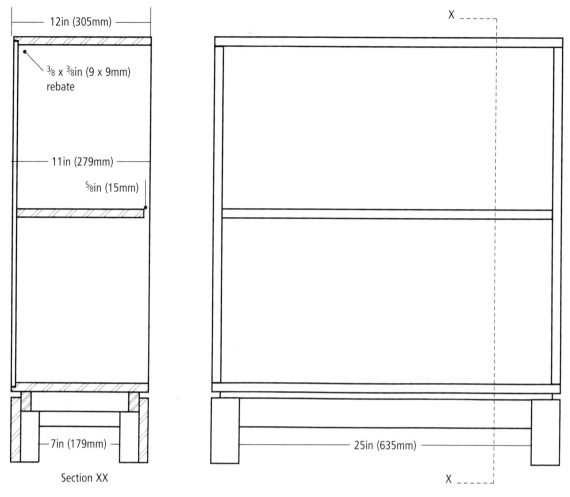

12in (305mm)

³⁄₈ x ³⁄₈in (9 x 9mm) rebate

11in (279mm)

⁵⁄₈in (15mm)

7in (179mm)

Section XX

X

25in (635mm)

X

FIG 17.2
Front view and side section with dimensions.

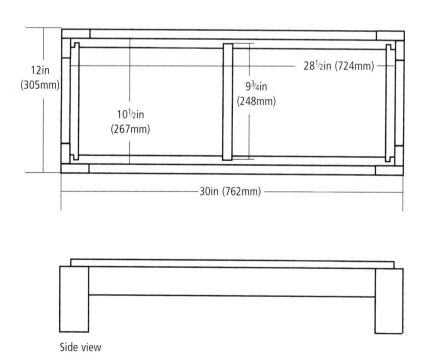

12in (305mm)

28½in (724mm)

9¾in (248mm)

10½in (267mm)

30in (762mm)

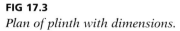

Side view

FIG 17.3
Plan of plinth with dimensions.

If the diagonals are not equal, loosen the sash cramps slightly, lay another sash cramp across the long diagonal and tighten it until the diagonals of the frame are the same length. Leaving this clamp in position, re-tighten the other clamps. When set clean off all the glue and plane the outside of the frame flat (see Fig 17.4).

3 Cut the rails for the inner stand to size. Join the corners with bare-faced housing joints, and fit the cross rail in the centre of the long rails with a simple housing joint (see page 20). Before gluing the joints together, drill and countersink a series of screw holes in the rails both to join the inner stand to the outer stand and to join the inner stand to the carcass after it has been made.

FIG 17.4
Cleaning up the outside of the outer frame.

FIG 17.5
The finished plinth with the inner and outer frames joined together.

4 Assemble the inner stand dry and fit it into the outer stand to check for accuracy of the fit. Adjust if required. Glue and screw the inner stand to the outer stand, with ½in (12mm) protruding from the top of the outer stand (see Fig 17.5).

CARCASS

1 Cut all the carcass pieces to size and join the corners with box joints (see page 17). To save time, and to help with the accuracy of the finished joint, make a plywood template from which to mark out the joints.

(While the boards are lying around between joints being cut, store them flat with a few weights on top to ensure that they do not bend or warp. Once jointed and glued this will not happen, but it helps if they are stored flat beforehand.)

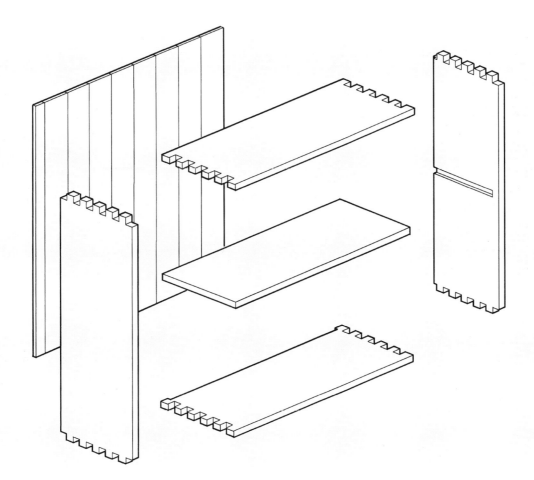

FIG 17.6
Carcass construction.

2 Rebate the back inside edges of the four sides of the carcass to a depth of ⅜in (9mm) with a router, to house the back. These are stopped rebates on the top and base, and through rebates on the two sides. Cut a housing joint in each side to accommodate the shelf (see page 20).

3 Glue and clamp the carcass and check it for squareness, then clean up the outside of the carcass with a plane. Cut the shelf to size and cut out the notches from the front edge. Glue the shelf into place in the carcass.

4 The back could be made from pine or plywood. Here, ⅜in (9mm) thick pine cladding was chosen. Cut the planks to the correct length, fit them into the back, and secure with pins and glue. They are fixed using a technique of 'secret' nailing, where the pins are put into the tongue part of the boards as the boards are put into place one at a time. The head of the pin is concealed in the tongue when the groove of the next plank to be placed into position is pushed over the tongue that contains the pin (see Fig 17.7).

ASSEMBLY AND FINISHING

1 Screw and glue the plinth to the carcass (see Fig 17.8).

2 Apply three coats of clear matt polyurethane varnish to match the desk and chair from Chapters 14 and 15.

FIG 17.7
Pinning the planks into the carcass to form the back.

FIG 17.8
Securing the plinth to the carcass with screws.

About the author

Since giving up his day job in the electronics pre-press industry, Dave Mackenzie now divides his time between lecturing – on graphic design, DTP and magazine journalism – and woodworking.

This is his first book, following a couple of hundred magazine articles on woodworking and DIY published over the last 20 years. These articles range from furniture design to kite making and much else in between.

Dave Mackenzie is married with two children and enjoys painting, walking and twitching.

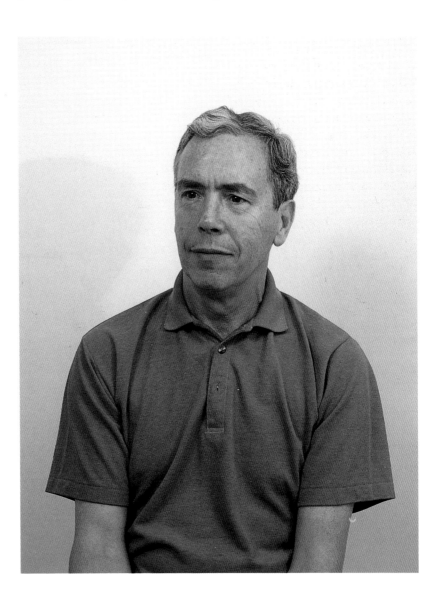

Index

WOODWORKING

40 More Woodworking Plans & Projects	*GMC Publications*
Bird Boxes and Feeders for the Garden	*Dave Mackenzie*
Complete Woodfinishing	*Ian Hosker*
Electric Woodwork	*Jeremy Broun*
Furniture & Cabinetmaking Projects	*GMC Publications*
Furniture Projects	*Rod Wales*
Furniture Restoration (Practical Crafts)	*Kevin Jan Bonner*
Furniture Restoration and Repair for Beginners	*Kevin Jan Bonner*
Green Woodwork	*Mike Abbott*
The Incredible Router	*Jeremy Broun*
Making & Modifying Woodworking Tools	*Jim Kingshott*
Making Chairs and Tables	*GMC Publications*
Making Fine Furniture	*Tom Darby*
Making Little Boxes from Wood	*John Bennett*
Making Shaker Furniture	*Barry Jackson*
Pine Furniture Projects for the Home	*Dave Mackenzie*
The Router and Furniture & Cabinetmaking Test Reports	*GMC Publications*
Sharpening Pocket Reference Book	*Jim Kingshott*
Sharpening: The Complete Guide	*Jim Kingshott*
Space-Saving Furniture Projects	*Dave Mackenzie*
Stickmaking: A Complete Course	*Andrew Jones & Clive George*
Veneering: A Complete Course	*Ian Hosker*
Woodfinishing Handbook (Practical Crafts)	*Ian Hosker*
Woodworking Plans and Projects	*GMC Publications*
The Workshop	*Jim Kingshott*

WOODTURNING

Adventures in Woodturning	*David Springett*
Bert Marsh: Woodturner	*Bert Marsh*
Bill Jones' Notes from the Turning Shop	*Bill Jones*
Bill Jones' Further Notes from the Turning Shop	*Bill Jones*
Colouring Techniques for Woodturners	*Jan Sanders*
The Craftsman Woodturner	*Peter Child*
Decorative Techniques for Woodturners	*Hilary Bowen*
Essential Tips for Woodturners	*GMC Publications*
Faceplate Turning	*GMC Publications*
Fun at the Lathe	*R.C. Bell*
Illustrated Woodturning Techniques	*John Hunnex*
Intermediate Woodturning Projects	*GMC Publications*
Keith Rowley's Woodturning Projects	*Keith Rowley*
Make Money from Woodturning	*Ann & Bob Phillips*
Multi-Centre Woodturning	*Ray Hopper*
Pleasure and Profit from Woodturning	*Reg Sherwin*
Practical Tips for Turners & Carvers	*GMC Publications*
Practical Tips for Woodturners	*GMC Publications*
Spindle Turning	*GMC Publications*
Turning Miniatures in Wood	*John Sainsbury*
Turning Wooden Toys	*Terry Lawrence*
Understanding Woodturning	*Ann & Bob Phillips*
Useful Techniques for Woodturners	*GMC Publications*
Useful Woodturning Projects	*GMC Publications*
Woodturning: A Foundation Course	*Keith Rowley*
Woodturning: A Source Book of Shapes	*John Hunnex*
Woodturning Jewellery	*Hilary Bowen*
Woodturning Masterclass	*Tony Boase*
Woodturning Techniques	*GMC Publications*
Woodturning Tools & Equipment Test Reports	*GMC Publications*
Woodturning Wizardry	*David Springett*

WOODCARVING

The Art of the Woodcarver	*GMC Publications*
Carving Birds & Beasts	*GMC Publications*
Carving on Turning	*Chris Pye*
Carving Realistic Birds	*David Tippey*
Decorative Woodcarving	*Jeremy Williams*
Essential Tips for Woodcarvers	*GMC Publications*
Essential Woodcarving Techniques	*Dick Onians*
Lettercarving in Wood: A Practical Course	*Chris Pye*
Practical Tips for Turners & Carvers	*GMC Publications*
Relief Carving in Wood: A Practical Introduction	*Chris Pye*
Understanding Woodcarving	*GMC Publications*
Understanding Woodcarving in the Round	*GMC Publications*
Useful Techniques for Woodcarvers	*GMC Publications*
Wildfowl Carving - Volume 1	*Jim Pearce*
Wildfowl Carving - Volume 2	*Jim Pearce*
The Woodcarvers	*GMC Publications*
Woodcarving: A Complete Course	*Ron Butterfield*
Woodcarving: A Foundation Course	*Zoë Gertner*
Woodcarving for Beginners	*GMC Publications*
Woodcarving Tools & Equipment Test Reports	*GMC Publications*
Woodcarving Tools, Materials & Equipment	*Chris Pye*

UPHOLSTERY

Seat Weaving (Practical Crafts)	*Ricky Holdstock*
Upholsterer's Pocket Reference Book	*David James*
Upholstery: A Complete Course	*David James*
Upholstery Restoration	*David James*
Upholstery Techniques & Projects	*David James*

TOYMAKING

Designing & Making Wooden Toys	*Terry Kelly*	Restoring Rocking Horses	*Clive Green & Anthony Dew*
Fun to Make Wooden Toys & Games	*Jeff & Jennie Loader*	Scrollsaw Toy Projects	*Ivor Carlyle*
Making Board, Peg & Dice Games	*Jeff & Jennie Loader*	Wooden Toy Projects	*GMC Publications*
Making Wooden Toys & Games	*Jeff & Jennie Loader*		

DOLLS' HOUSES AND MINIATURES

Architecture for Dolls' Houses	*Joyce Percival*	Making Period Dolls' House Accessories	*Andrea Barham*
Beginners' Guide to the Dolls' House Hobby	*Jean Nisbett*	Making Period Dolls' House Furniture	*Derek & Sheila Rowbottom*
The Complete Dolls' House Book	*Jean Nisbett*	Making Tudor Dolls' Houses	*Derek Rowbottom*
Dolls' House Accessories, Fixtures and Fittings	*Andrea Barham*	Making Unusual Miniatures	*Graham Spalding*
Dolls' House Bathrooms: Lots of Little Loos	*Patricia King*	Making Victorian Dolls' House Furniture	*Patricia King*
Easy to Make Dolls' House Accessories	*Andrea Barham*	Miniature Bobbin Lace	*Roz Snowden*
Make Your Own Dolls' House Furniture	*Maurice Harper*	Miniature Embroidery for the Victorian Dolls' House	*Pamela Warner*
Making Dolls' House Furniture	*Patricia King*	Miniature Needlepoint Carpets	*Janet Granger*
Making Georgian Dolls' Houses	*Derek Rowbottom*	The Secrets of the Dolls' House Makers	*Jean Nisbett*
Making Miniature Oriental Rugs & Carpets	*Meik & Ian McNaughton*		

CRAFTS

American Patchwork Designs in Needlepoint	*Melanie Tacon*	Embroidery Tips & Hints	*Harold Hayes*
A Beginners' Guide to Rubber Stamping	*Brenda Hunt*	An Introduction to Crewel Embroidery	*Mave Glenny*
Celtic Knotwork Designs	*Sheila Sturrock*	Making Character Bears	*Valerie Tyler*
Collage from Seeds, Leaves and Flowers	*Joan Carver*	Making Greetings Cards for Beginners	*Pat Sutherland*
Complete Pyrography	*Stephen Poole*	Making Knitwear Fit	*Pat Ashforth & Steve Plummer*
Creating Knitwear Designs	*Pat Ashforth & Steve Plummer*	Needlepoint: A Foundation Course	*Sandra Hardy*
Creative Embroidery Techniques		Pyrography Handbook (Practical Crafts)	*Stephen Poole*
Using Colour Through Gold	*Daphne J. Ashby & Jackie Woolsey*	Tassel Making for Beginners	*Enid Taylor*
Cross Stitch Kitchen Projects	*Janet Granger*	Tatting Collage	*Lindsay Rogers*
Cross Stitch on Colour	*Sheena Rogers*	Temari: A Traditional Japanese Embroidery Technique	*Margaret Ludlow*

THE HOME

Home Ownership: Buying and Maintaining	*Nicholas Snelling*	Security for the Householder: Fitting Locks and Other Devices	*E. Phillips*

VIDEOS

Drop-in and Pinstuffed Seats	*David James*	Twists and Advanced Turning	*Dennis White*
Stuffover Upholstery	*David James*	Sharpening the Professional Way	*Jim Kingshott*
Elliptical Turning	*David Springett*	Sharpening Turning & Carving Tools	*Jim Kingshott*
Woodturning Wizardry	*David Springett*	Bowl Turning	*John Jordan*
Turning Between Centres: The Basics	*Dennis White*	Hollow Turning	*John Jordan*
Turning Bowls	*Dennis White*	Woodturning: A Foundation Course	*Keith Rowley*
Boxes, Goblets and Screw Threads	*Dennis White*	Carving a Figure: The Female Form	*Ray Gonzalez*
Novelties and Projects	*Dennis White*	The Router: A Beginner's Guide	*Alan Goodsell*
Classic Profiles	*Dennis White*	The Scroll Saw: A Beginner's Guide	*John Burke*

MAGAZINES

Woodturning • Woodcarving • Furniture & Cabinetmaking • The Router
The Dolls' House Magazine • Creative Crafts for the Home • BusinessMatters

The above represents a full list of all titles currently published or scheduled to be published. All are available direct from the Publishers or through bookshops, newsagents and specialist retailers. To place an order, or to obtain a complete catalogue, contact:

GMC Publications, 166 High Street, Lewes, East Sussex BN7 1XU, United Kingdom
Tel: 01273 488005 Fax: 01273 478606

Orders by credit card are accepted